# WHY I SHOULD WORK FOR YOU?

# Visit our How To website at www.howto.co.uk

At **www.howto.co.uk** you can engage in conversation with our authors - all of whom have 'been there and done that' in their specialist fields. You can get access to special offers and additional content but most importantly you will be able to engage with, and become a part of, a wide and growing community of people just like yourself.

At **www.howto.co.uk** you'll be able to talk and share tips with people who have similar interests and are facing similar challenges in their lives. People who, just like you, have the desire to change their lives for the better - be it through moving to a new country, starting a new business, growing their own vegetables, or writing a novel.

At **www.howto.co.uk** you'll find the support and encouragement you need to help make your aspirations a reality.

**How To Books** strives to present authentic, inspiring, practical information in their books.  Now, when you buy a title from **How To Books**, you get even more than just words on a page.

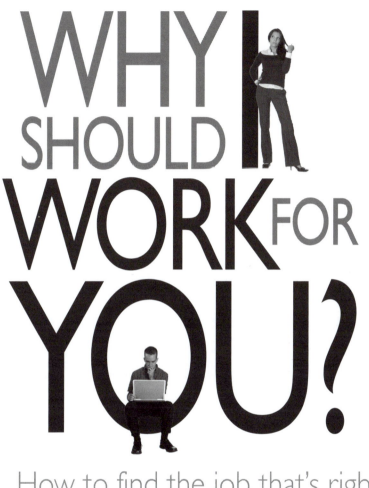

# WHY
## SHOULD
# WORK FOR
# YOU?

How to find the job that's right
for you – and get the offer

## KEITH POTTS & JASON DEIGN

**howto**books

Published by How To Books Ltd,
Spring Hill House, Spring Hill Road
Begbroke, Oxford OX5 1RX, United Kingdom.
Tel: (01865) 375794  Fax: (01865) 379162
info@howtobooks.co.uk
www.howtobooks.co.uk

British Library Cataloguing in Publication Data.
A catalogue record for this book is available from the British Library.

ISBN: 978 1 84528 347 6

Cover design by Baseline Arts Ltd
Produced for How To Books by Deer Park Productions, Tavistock
Typeset by Baseline Arts Ltd, Oxford
Printed and bound in Great Britain by Cromwell Press Group, Trowbridge, Wiltshire

NOTE: The material contained in this book is set out in good faith for general guidance and no liability can be accepted for loss or expense incurred as a result of relying in particular circumstances on statements made in this book. Laws and regulations are complex and liable to change, and readers should check the current position with the relevant authorities before making personal arrangements.

# Contents

# Acknowledgements

THE authors would like to thank all the people who provided time and knowledge in helping to create this book. The idea behind it was originally put forward by Rafe Offer, whose help thereafter has been indispensable in making sure it could see the light of day. Particular mentions should also go to Marianne Craig, who very generously agreed to allow us to use elements of her excellent Firework career coaching programme throughout the text, and to Michelle Bayley, whose contributions to the Jobsite website formed the basis for much of our discussion on how to improve your knowledge of yourself and your work priorities.

Many thanks also to David Moxon for his invaluable advice on what to do and what not to do in interviews, Philip Landau for his pointers on what to watch out for in work contracts, Wayne Clarke for being a willing case study in chapter 2 and Lizzie Bentley-Bowers for her career counselling help. Chapter 10 could not have been written without the input provided by Scott McNaughton and Irena Molloy of BDO Stoy Hayward, Sally Cohen of Elizabeth Arden (UK), and Kevin Bohan of Diageo.

Throughout the text we have also drawn on published commentary and research, the providers of which we gratefully acknowledge. And finally we are forever indebted to the superlative assistance provided by Susanna Davidson, Vicky Taylor and Cheryl Morgan at Jobsite.

# Think about your job

In any case, the detail is there for illustration only. The central premise of this book is not dependent on any single fact or statistic. We hope you find this premise interesting. We hope it moves you to think about your current situation. We hope it moves you to act. Best of luck with your new life at work.

*"The central premise of this book is not dependent on any single fact or statistic."*

# What you'll get out of this book

- Tools to help you work out what you need in a job to make you happier and more fulfilled.
- Tips on making your current job work better for you
- The secret to going after the job you want and getting it
- The key to securing interviews and performing well at them
- Advice on getting the best possible deal from a new employer

# Preface

IS this book for you? Most likely. If you're in employment, or thinking about being in employment, then the chances are you'll find this book useful. Given the broad potential appeal of its subject matter, we have tried to keep the text as simple and straightforward as possible. At the same time, though, we would like to think that the central theme of this volume is, well, slightly radical. So some of you might need a bit of convincing.

## Give me the facts

For such people, and indeed for those who are simply curious, we have included the drier, more factual information, such as sources, percentages, dates and whatnot, as footnotes to each page. We have tried to include the latest information available at the time of writing. But trends and statistics change all the time and some of the detailed figures in this book will undoubtedly be out of date by the time you read it, for which we can only apologise.

We also apologise for any references taken from the internet in which the links we have quoted no longer work; that is down to the ever-changing nature of the web and is not something over which we have much control. Finally, this is a subject that gets surveyed a lot, and in some cases the findings are somewhat conflicting because the job market evolves so rapidly. We have done our best to pick figures which represent the general consensus, where there is one, but it's entirely likely that you may hear something completely different from another source.

CHAPTER 1:

# Happy@Work?

**What you'll get out of this chapter:**
- A 10-minute test that will tell you whether you've got a good or bad deal at work.
- A valuable new way of looking at your relationship with your employer.
- A 10-point plan to achieving happiness at work.

## ARE you happy at work?

No need to answer straight away. Take your time.

After all, work is taking up *your* time. Nine to five (at least). Five days a week (at least). Most of your adult life (at least). Shouldn't you be doing something in that time that you are happy with … at least?

So … are you happy? If the answer is: 'yes, definitely', then great; why are you reading this book? If the answer is: 'no, definitely not' (or if you're currently out of work and looking for a job) then skip this chapter and head straight to the next one, where we'll start helping you to achieve a better life. But if your answer is: 'err, hmm, not sure…', then let's find out for real in the next ten minutes.

## TAKE THE HAPPY DAYS TEST

What you're about to do is called the Happy Days test. It won't tell you if you're The Fonz[1], but it will reveal how much satisfaction you're getting out of work — and what the problem areas are. The test was devised by a leading psychologist, David Moxon, who is an associate lecturer at Anglia Ruskin University and head of the Psychology Department at Peterborough Regional College. It will help you understand how your work life and

*"...for almost half of the population, having a bad day at work can have a bad effect on their health and home life..."*

---

1. In case you were born after the mid-eighties, this is a reference to an American sitcom.

home life fit together, which is important because for almost half of the population, having a bad day at work can have a bad effect on their health and home life[2].

How does it work? Simple. We'll give you ten sets of four statements. For each set, pick a statement that you think most closely matches how you feel and jot down the score next to it. Then go through the same statements again, but this time pretend to be someone who knows you well — your partner or best friend, say — and pick the ones which you think *they* would choose on your behalf[3]. If you get stuck, don't worry: just head to *www.jobsite.co.uk/happydays* for a simple, free online version that will do all the calculating for you.

Ready to start? Good! Then let's go.

| | How I feel about work | How my best friend or partner thinks I feel |
|---|---|---|
| **Section 1: CONTROL** | | |
| I don't feel valued or appreciated | 1 | 1 |
| I feel very valued and appreciated | 3 | 3 |
| My company doesn't value my views | 2 | 2 |
| I'm in charge of my work, I feel in control, I rarely feel swamped by other people's demands on my time | 4 | 4 |
| **Section 2: STRESS** | | |
| I find my work boring | 2 | 2 |
| Work gives me 'a real buzz' | 4 | 4 |
| I dread going to work in the morning | 1 | 1 |
| I enjoy the challenge of my work | 3 | 3 |
| **Section 3: MONEY** | | |
| I have so much money | 4 | 4 |
| I enjoy spending money on family and friends | 3 | 3 |
| My leisure/family suffers because I have no money | 2 | 2 |
| Lack of money makes me miserable at home | 1 | 1 |

2. Specifically, 46% of people say a bad day impacts negatively on their health and home life.
3. No, we don't know how or why it works, either. But you'll find it's unnervingly accurate.

|  | How I feel about work | How my best friend or partner thinks I feel |
|---|---|---|
| **Section 4: CREATIVITY** | | |
| My work allows me to be creative | 3 | 3 |
| Work really stifles my creative side | 1 | 1 |
| My work doesn't allow me to be creative | 2 | 2 |
| I have a really creative job | 4 | 4 |
| **Section 5: HAPPINESS** | | |
| I'm very happy at work | 4 | 4 |
| Work makes me so miserable | 1 | 1 |
| My friendships with my colleagues make work fine | 3 | 3 |
| Work tends to bring my mood down | 2 | 2 |
| **Section 6: MONEY** | | |
| My salary is low for the amount of effort I put into work | 2 | 2 |
| I can't survive on the salary I earn | 1 | 1 |
| Working makes me very rich | 4 | 4 |
| I feel I earn a fair wage | 3 | 3 |
| **Section 7: CONTROL** | | |
| I don't get enough time to spend with my family/friends | 2 | 2 |
| My work/life balance is brilliant | 4 | 4 |
| There is not enough time in the week for leisure/fun | 1 | 1 |
| I don't need to take my work home with me | 3 | 3 |
| **Section 8: STRESS** | | |
| On the whole, my family really stresses me | 1 | 1 |
| I can really unwind at home | 3 | 3 |
| I generally find my leisure time boring | 2 | 2 |
| My home life is lots of fun | 4 | 4 |

| | How I feel about work | How my best friend or partner thinks I feel |
|---|---|---|
| **Section 9: CREATIVITY** | | |
| I have time to be creative outside work | 3 | 3 |
| My home life is very predictable and boring | 1 | 1 |
| My leisure time lacks imagination | 2 | 2 |
| My leisure pursuits are highly creative (I try to do something different and unusual, such as painting, rock climbing, belly dancing …) | 4 | 4 |
| **Section 10: HAPPINESS** | | |
| Not being at work makes me happy | 3 | 3 |
| Having leisure time makes me very miserable | 1 | 1 |
| I am really happy with my home life | 4 | 4 |
| I can't wait to get back to work after a holiday | 2 | 2 |

## How did you score?

Use the table below to jot down the numbers you circled for each section - both the one that you selected and the one that you thought someone close to you would have picked.

| SECTION | SCORE 1 | SCORE 2 |
|---|---|---|
| 1. Control | | |
| 2. Stress | | |
| 3. Money | | |
| 4. Creativity | | |
| 5. Happiness | | |
| 6. Money | | |
| 7. Control | | |
| 8. Stress | | |
| 9. Creativity | | |
| 10. Happiness | | |
| *Totals:* | | |

Add up all the numbers in the 'score 1' column and then do the same for the 'score 2' column so that you have a total figure for both. Your scores for each column should be somewhere between 10 and 40. Check your scores against the chart below and then turn to the page shown for your Happy Days test results. This will tell you how you really feel about your work. Plus we've included more detailed feedback in the Appendix 1 at the end of the book. But first, let's see how you scored:

| Column 1 score: | Column 2 score: | Score category: | Turn to page: |
| --- | --- | --- | --- |
| 31 to 40 | 31 to 40 | High-High | 5 |
| 31 to 40 | 21 to 30 | High-Medium | 6 |
| 31 to 40 | 10 to 20 | High-Low | 6 |
| 21 to 30 | 31 to 40 | Medium-High | 6 |
| 21 to 30 | 21 to 30 | Medium-Medium | 7 |
| 21 to 30 | 10 to 20 | Medium-Low | 7 |
| 10 to 20 | 31 to 40 | Low-High | 7 |
| 10 to 20 | 21 to 30 | Low-Medium | 8 |
| 10 to 20 | 10 to 20 | Low-Low | 8 |

**If your scores are High-High (31-40 and 31-40)**
You're really happy in your work. Great! Your work life has an impact on your life outside the normal nine to five, and in your case it should be a positive one.

*" Your work life has an impact on your life outside the normal nine to five."*

Take a good look at your detailed feedback (in the appendix) to see what areas significantly contribute to your happiness so you can try and keep them that way. Also have a think about whether any of these areas are only temporary. You may love the fact that your workload is easy to manage at the moment … but in a few months will you be frustrated that you're not being challenged?

If some areas do become less than ideal, don't be afraid to act quickly and head off any negativity. Many people are unhappy at work; make sure you don't become one of them. If you can find ways to make your work life better, your whole life will work better.

### If your scores are High-Medium (31-40 and 21-30)

You claim to be happy in your work … but perhaps that's not the whole truth. It could be that, deep down, you're not as well paid as you think you deserve to be, or you're unhappy with how your boss interferes in your work. Turn to the appendix for more detailed feedback and think carefully about whether you need to make a change in your work or life, and in what area.

Many people think being unhappy with elements of work is part and parcel of having a job, but they're wrong. You don't have to put up with things you're not happy with. A minor grumble now could easily escalate if you don't deal with it, or could start to affect other parts of your life. Don't be afraid to address problems, however minor you like to think they are. You alone have the power to change your work and life.

### If your scores are High-Low (31-40 and 10-20)

You claim to be happy in your work. But that seems to be far from the truth. Although you tell yourself all is well, some things appear to be dragging you down. It could be that you're not as well paid as you think you deserve to be, but you feel it's a sign of greed to complain about money. Or maybe you like to give the impression all is well in your job, even to yourself, when in fact you're drowning in a sea of paperwork. Don't suffer in silence and don't stubbornly decide to sit it out.

Research has shown that being unhappy at work can be bad for your physical and mental health. Head to the appendix for more detailed feedback and think about where you need to take action. Whatever happens, don't fail to address problems like this. You owe it to yourself and it's your right to be happy at work.

### If your scores are Medium-High (21-30 and 31-40)

Although you feel work can sometimes be a grind, in fact you have a lot to be happy about. Cheer up! Research has shown that being happy in your work has a real, positive impact on your health and wellbeing, for instance.

Take a look at the detailed feedback in the appendix, work out which areas make you happier than you let on … and embrace them.

Most importantly, if you've got a downer on work then make sure it doesn't become a self-fulfilling prophecy. Without realising it, being less than upbeat about how happy work makes you could wear away the real positive feelings it gives you.

> *"Without realising it, being less than upbeat about how happy work makes you could wear away the real positive feelings it gives you."*

### If your scores are Medium-Medium (21-30 and 21-30)

Work is so-so. You may not lie awake on Sunday nights, dreading the morning, but nor do you particularly look forward to Mondays. You're not actively unhappy but you feel that you could be happier in many ways. Maybe you're resigned to the fact that work will be faintly unfulfilling. Maybe you see it as a means to an end and nothing more. Be careful. There is a risk that things could easily slump and leave you feeling actively unhappy.

It doesn't have to be this way. Take a look at our detailed feedback in the appendix and find ways to make things more positive. Your whole life will benefit.

### If your scores are Medium-Low (21-30 and 10-20)

You may pretend to yourself that work is so-so. But you're far less happy than you will admit. However, work doesn't have to be this way. Take a look at the detailed feedback in the appendix and then act on it. A few simple changes may make a big difference to your happiness.

### If your scores are Low-High (10-20 and 31-40)

You feel work can sometimes be a grind. But in fact you've a lot to be happy about. So why the long face? Are you drawing unfair comparisons between yourself and other people? Most of us want different things out of our life and therefore our work, so judge yourself on what you want, not on what others believe you should have.

> *"Judge yourself on what you want, not on what others believe you should have."*

As well as taking a more realistic view of your situation, you might want to check the detailed feedback in the appendix and see what areas make your life go so well, so you can try to keep them that way.

### If your scores are Low-Medium (10-20 and 21-30)

Okay, so things are less than ideal. Maybe it's your pay. Maybe it's your boss. But the chances are you could do with a change. Head straight to the appendix at the back of this book to find out what areas are causing the most problems, and how to fix them.

### If your scores are Low-Low (10-20 and 10-20)

You probably don't need us to tell you this, but you're deeply unhappy in your work. You need to make a change for the better, and soon. Whatever aspects of your work are making you unhappy, remember that it has an impact on your whole life. Research has shown that being unhappy at work can have a real, negative impact on your health. Make sure things don't stay this way. Read the detailed feedback in the appendix, think about where you can most easily make a change for the better, and take action. Do it now.

## TOWARDS GREATER HAPPINESS

By now you should have a much clearer idea of your real relationship with your work, and (if you've checked the appendix) pointers on what specific areas of your job and your life might need improving. Your life is too short and too precious to waste on work which isn't making you happy, so hopefully you'll agree the next step is to look at ways of improving your lot. But before we do that, let's just review your relationship with work. And to start, stand in front of the mirror. Picture yourself in your boss's office. Now ask: 'Why should I work for you?' What kind of answer do you imagine coming back at you? Is it enough?

Think about this. It's really important. If you work in an average job in the United Kingdom, you probably get about five weeks off a year. If you work an eight-hour day (you wish ...) then that's 1,880 hours a year you're spending at work. Or around 64% of your working life. Now ask the question again. Are you spending more than half of your life doing something that is not fulfilling? And if so ... why?

*"Are you spending more than half of your life doing something that is not fulfilling? And if so... why?"*

Fortunately we no longer live in the Dark Ages when it comes to employment. Rather than ploughing fields or slaving in mines, you can choose to wizard up websites or cook cordon bleu. If you dreamt of being a nurse or a fireman as a kid, nowadays there is very little preventing you from fulfilling that dream as an adult. But wanting it is rarely enough. You have to take action.

*Tip: Think about all the people you know of. Which ones have fancy jobs? Work in TV, for example, or travel the world as a big-shot consultant, or rule the roost in a large company boardroom? Which ones have flashy cars, a really good take-home salary, a second home? Which ones get to enjoy work and have loads of time off, travelling or being with their family? Which ones live abroad, soaking up the sun while you slave away in a dingy office? And what sets them apart from you, other than maybe a little ambition, a bit of graft or a few smart decisions at the right time? If you've ever thought 'I could do that', do you owe it to yourself to start thinking 'and why not?'*

These days there are really very few occupations that are not open to almost anyone. Becoming a world-class athlete or artist clearly requires exceptional ability. Becoming an astronaut takes a lot of luck and dedication. But as for almost anything else ... well, the field is open and the sky is the limit. And increasingly for many people 'the job' is just part of a much wider and more important package, 'the life', which includes more time off, greater flexibility, an improved work-life balance and so on. For you, too, there are more options now than ever before. Shouldn't you be taking advantage?

## WHAT IS ALL YOUR CURRENT EFFORT FOR ANYWAY?

After all, if you don't do your job for love and fulfilment, what are you doing it for? Maybe it's not the work, but the people. But how do you know these people are going to stick around? If they aren't too keen on things, either, the chances are they will ship out sooner or later. If you move, you could simply make an effort to keep in touch with your old friends, make new ones too … and be better off into the bargain.

> *"If you don't do your job for love and fulfilment, what are you doing it for?"*

## MORE THAN MONEY

Is it the money that is making your current work worthwhile? Sure, you get paid to work, but is it enough? Is it as much as you need? Or as much as you would like? This is a wild guess, but we suspect the answer to at least one of these questions is 'no'. And, as mentioned earlier, for many people the rewards they get out of life are not financial ones. They are to do with spending more time with their family, having the ability to spend time on sports or hobbies, and so on. Is your job giving you the money *and* the freedom to enjoy life?

Finally, what about stability? For some, the comfort of a regular pay cheque and a familiar work environment seemingly outweighs the benefits of leaving for something better. But just how secure is your job? Go back 30 or 40 years, to your mum and dad's generation, and maybe you could expect a job for life. One where you started off as an apprentice and left the company 60 years later with a gold watch and a comfy pension. But when was the last time you heard of one of those nowadays?

Overall, almost 2 out of 10 people in the public and private sectors across the United Kingdom leave work every year for one reason or another[4], but this level is higher in the private sector[5]. Admittedly a lot of this turnover is down to people opting to leave rather than being pushed out, but in any case it's clearly a bit fanciful to think that any job today can provide you with real stability in the long term.

## GO-GETTER OR DEAD-ENDER?

If you're not in your job for fun, money or stability, what are you in it for? This is a question a lot of people could be asking right now. In a survey called 'Happiness at Work', carried out among 1000 respondents by Badenoch & Clark, a recruitment agency, almost a quarter of white collar workers in the United Kingdom said they were unhappy in their jobs[6]. These findings tally with other research. When Jobsite.co.uk, the online recruitment website, surveyed 5000 workers across the United Kingdom, it found that nearly half of them don't like work and 3 out of 10 would leave just like that if given a better option. But interestingly, much fewer actually do leave.

*"If you're not in your job for fun, money or stability, what are you in it for?"*

# Maybe they should start looking.

## SHOW YOUR INITIATIVE

With 'jobs for life' a thing of the past, employers will always be keen to take on people who can show they have drive and initiative. And one of the ways you demonstrate that is by leaving employers who don't measure up. A well-paid executive nowadays will likely as not have a CV that reads a bit like a who's who of the corporate world.

4. Actually 17.3%, according to the 2008 annual survey report on recruitment, retention and turnover from the Chartered Institute of Personnel and Development.
5. 20.4%, from the same survey.
6. The survey was carried out in May 2007 using Tickbox.net, an online polling service, and was widely reported in the British press, including references in the *Guardian* ('Quarter of UK office staff "unhappy"', 15 May, 2007) and BBC News Online ('UK office staff "unhappy at work"', 15 May, 2007).

They will have travelled widely around the islands of industry and collected valuable experiences and contacts. Many will have worked outside the United Kingdom. Each job change will not have harmed them, but made them stronger, more valuable, more sought after. They will have demonstrated to the world that they know what they want, they go out to get it, and if they cannot find it where they are, then they will look elsewhere. By the same token, there is more respect and appreciation nowadays for people who want to achieve a better balance between their jobs and the rest of their lives.

*"With 'jobs for life' a thing of the past, employers will always be keen to take on people who can show they have drive and initiative."*

Employers increasingly recognise that these people might be more loyal, more productive, more motivated, and ultimately do a better job than colleagues whose backs are smarting from the crack of a corporate whip.

## PRIZE RECRUITS

Every business in the country values these experienced go-getters, these confident self-starters, these ambitious corporate drivers and these balanced hard-workers who like or even love their jobs. You could be one of them. There really is not much stopping you looking for another opportunity. But it's not going to happen to you if you insist on burying your head in the sand. And you cannot count on the perfect job to just come knocking on your door, either.

In a survey of 868 employers across the country[7], 8 out of 10 said the main objective of their employment activities was to attract and recruit key staff to the organisation. They call it the war for talent ... and you're the prize.

## CHANGING YOUR MINDSET

You have to change your mindset. Start thinking like an employer would think. If your current place of work does not measure up, fire it. Go out into

7. Published in the Chartered Institute of Personnel and Development's 2008 annual survey report of recruitment, retention and turnover.

the market and find one that does. Obviously you have to be careful. You're taking a serious step here and we wouldn't advocate jumping ship without something to go to. But if your current employer isn't right for you then start looking for one that is. Interview as many employers as you need. Check up on their credentials. Ask for references. Put your future employers through a rigorous selection process. Then, when you have found an employer you can work with, make sure you get them with the right terms and conditions. Keep them on their toes. Review their progress regularly. Benchmark them against other employers. If they show signs of slacking, get rid of them and get another new employer.

# Remember: now you're the boss.

## THE EMPLOYEE RULES

That's the long and short of it. It used to be that the customer was king. But then companies realised that taking care of customers was all down to their employees. So now the employee rules. Companies have not owned up to this in so many words, of course. But look carefully at how they behave and you will see it's true. Companies still need customers, but nowadays the chief executive is just as likely to bang on about how important their employees are, because … without them the organisation has nothing. Quite literally, its key assets walk out of the door every day at six o'clock.

## TEN STEPS TO THE DEAL JOB

Now you know where we are headed, the question is: how do we get there? In a nutshell, here are the steps you need to take:

1.  Assess your current work situation to see if it's satisfactory, and if not, why not? We did this earlier on with the Happy Days test.

2.  Sort out your short-, mid- and long-term career goals and see if you can make changes that will help you move towards the work you want. We cover this in Chapter 2.

3. Work out what sort of job would suit you better. It's vital that you find the right match, and in Chapter 3 we give you a unique tool to do this.

4. Before you leave your job, it's always worth seeing how you can improve your current situation. This is what Chapter 4 is all about.

5. If you cannot improve your current lot, then you need to start drawing up a list of potential 'employer suitors' and approach them about work. More of this in Chapter 5.

6. Create a plan of attack, and a suitable arsenal of written information, to catch the eye of the employer you want. For this, see Chapter 6.

7. Create the right impression at interview and know how to answer every question thrown at you. See Chapters 7 and 8.

8. Land the job, check that it really is the thing you're looking for, and make sure you get the best possible deal from your new employer. See Chapter 9.

9. Understand how leading employers attract talent and how you can get on their radar. We take a look at this in chapter 10.

10. Review your short-, mid- and long- term goals as you go through life, to make sure your work aspirations match your changing lifestyle (Chapter 11).

# That, then, is the plan. Ready to get started? Then let's go.

CHAPTER 2:
# Who you are and what you want

*What you'll get out of this chapter:*
- ■ *Ten things to ask yourself to find out what you risk losing if you leave your job.*
- ■ *Six ways to improve your knowledge of yourself.*
- ■ *Three questions to help you find out what your true values are.*

MEET Wayne Clarke. Early thirties. Lives with his wife and child in a nice house in a nice part of London. Wears a smart suit to work and believes in making a good impression on the people he meets. Softly-spoken, charismatic, down-to-earth, he is as at home talking to the chairman of the board as to the man on the street. As you will learn more about in the next chapter, his Jobsite personal profile is pure believer: he is continuously seeking new challenges and learning from them, coming up with ideas, taking risks and moving his career, and his life, forward with passion.

After college, Clarke joined a consultancy firm and worked in knowledge management, using intranets and other tools to help the firm's people make better use of the combined experience accumulated by the business. He quickly made his mark as someone who stood out from his peers. 'In consultancy there is a lot of hot air, a lot of talk, but not a lot of action', recalls one former colleague. 'Wayne wasn't like that. He wasn't into all the bullshit. He just got things done.'

## MOVING ON

Unsurprisingly, it wasn't long before Clarke moved on. He joined a large professional services practice with a brief to crank up internal communications. The business was growing rapidly and needed someone to make sure that the mass of new employees joining the firm would quickly get to grips with its values and strategic direction. Clarke not only overhauled the way the firm communicated with its employees, but helped it to break new ground entirely in the field of internal communications.

From staid PowerPoint slide shows and dry question-and-answer sessions, the firm's management, among whom Clarke was now seen as a trusted adviser, found itself taking part in interactive strategy-building sessions with video recordings, digital presentations, game-playing and more. The firm's investment in what it called 'employee engagement' ballooned more than 10-fold in a couple of years. It began to win awards for being the best employer in its sector. Clarke found himself being invited to talk about his ground-breaking approach around the country and around the world.

## JUST NOT ENOUGH

But it wasn't enough. 'Not long after I arrived, I started to feel there were other things I wanted to do', says Clarke. 'I convinced my employer to put me on a four-day-a-week work contract so that I could set up my own consultancy business and do other work on the side, but soon even that wasn't sufficient.' At the time of writing, Clarke is working for a successful UK entrepreneur, helping to set up a new global consultancy venture that will tap into a market worth millions.

*"Not long after I had arrived, I started to feel there were other things I wanted to do."*

## THE RIGHT MOVES

Throughout this career progression, Clarke's status and earning potential have increased steadily and significantly. But this is not a story about money or power. It is a story about getting what you want, what feels right for you. 'Being rewarded properly for what you do is always important, but it's not everything', says Clarke. 'Every time I've moved, it has been because I thought I could achieve more in my professional and personal life by doing so. And it has worked. Every time.'

There are two takeouts here. The first, is that Clarke's choices, the ones that led to this particular career progression, are typical of a believer. In Clarke's world view, anything is possible, including trying out completely new methods of internal communication or setting up global consultancy businesses aimed at new, untapped markets. And doing these things is worthwhile because of what they represent in themselves, not just because of the potential rewards they could bring.

# Had Clarke been a different type of worker, then his choices and his career progression would have been very different.

## YOU CAN DO IT

The second point to take out of Clarke's tale is that, no matter what his profile, if he hadn't chosen to move on at specific points of his career then he would never have got where he is today. And the chances are he would be a lot less happy.

## THE BEST OPTION

You see, there was nothing wrong in the work he was doing in previous roles; he was appreciated and well-rewarded by market standards. But the roles were not right for him, and even when he was putting 100% into them, he was not getting 100% back out. He was smart enough to realise that his best option was to move on, and that simple realisation has been the key to his success and happiness.

*Tip: Clearly, if you're going to ask your employer 'why should I work for you?', you have to be prepared for an unsatisfactory answer. And if you get one, are you prepared to move on? Frankly, it's not something we're all up to.*

*"If you're going to ask your employer 'why should I work for you?' you have to be prepared for an unsatisfactory answer."*

Now it's time to take a more considered view of the risks involved in moving. Ask yourself the following questions:

1. **How does your job compare with others in similar positions?**
2. **How much is it giving you? Is it rewarding and is it rewarding in the ways that matter? How much of the things that matter to you does your job provide? (For this, don't forget to check your worker personality profile in Chapter 3.)**
3. **How much are you giving it? What is your commitment to your job in terms of hours worked, going beyond your job remit and so on?**
4. **How secure is your job?**
5. **Can you get what you want?**
6. **Could you get what you want elsewhere?**
7. **What things would you miss about your current job if you moved?**
8. **How much would you miss them?**
9. **Which of them would you definitely not be able to find elsewhere?**
10. **What things that really matter to you will you never be able to get in your current job?**
11. **What things that really matter to you would you be able to get elsewhere?**
12. **How easily would you be able to get them?**

It is important to bear in mind one thing here. You are not comparing your current job with the deal your colleagues, friends or family get. You are not comparing yourself with the industry average. These kinds of comparisons are fine if you're just looking to feel smug or feel sorry for yourself, but they won't help you find a job that is more suited to the kind of person that you are. Remember, what makes a job work for you will be different to what makes it work for anyone else. That is why the starting point for your analysis of your situation should be your worker profile.

# The best job in the world for a balancer will probably not be much use for a supporter.

Your profile will help you focus on the kinds of things that will matter, but beyond that there will be a host of factors that, like DNA, are unique to you. Whether you have debts, a mortgage, a family and so on will make a big difference to the amount of risk you're prepared to put up with. You will have likes and dislikes that will affect your career decisions. Your age, gender, beliefs, upbringing,

*"The only valid comparison to make is this: what have I got now? Versus what could I have elsewhere?"*

aspirations and experiences will all go into the melting pot when it comes to finding a job that suits you better. So, really, the only valid comparison to make is this: what have I got now? *Versus* what could I have elsewhere?

## BUT BEFORE YOU TAKE THE PLUNGE ...

There are a number of ways you can go about changing your career for the better but, in essence, if you're looking to create a meaningful, lasting change in your work life then it pays to put in a lot of thought and planning in advance. Michelle Bayley, a successful certified professional life and career coach[8], says: 'It helps to use exercises to get an awareness of who you are and what you want. Then you can start generating possibilities and creating a plan.'

## WHAT DO YOU WANT FROM LIFE?

'The first step is to find out what you want from work and from life in general. You cannot make meaningful choices about your career without looking at the life side too. You need to establish your values and review your personal and professional strengths and achievements, and get it all out of your head and down on paper. That way you can see what is really important to you.'

Bayley helps her clients through a programme called Firework, which was created by Marianne Craig and Kate Edmonds[9]. The key point about this and other career coaching programmes is that the process of going out and getting a new job is a relatively minor and late stage in the whole.

8.  Bayley's website is www.findyourwaycoaching.co.uk.
9.  See www.coachlifeandcareer.com and www.fireworkcoaching.com for more information. Many of the tools and techniques in this chapter are drawn from the Firework programme, and we are greatly indebted to both Michelle Bayley and Marianne Craig for their contributions and assistance with this section.

# The important part is to work out what you're looking for before you set out to find it.

Craig, an International Coaching Federation master certified coach, says: 'Research shows that those who are most satisfied and motivated by their work are in careers which reflect who they really are; careers which reflect their true nature and their real passions; careers which draw on their innate strengths and employ their favourite skills; and careers which allow them to honour their deeply-held values.'

## KNOW THYSELF

So the first step in improving your lot at work, it turns out, actually has very little to do with how you feel about work. Instead, it's to do with your inner self: the kind of person you are, your aspirations, your values and so on. You have already got some of this information from the previous chapter, but now it's time to dig deeper.

Michelle Bayley says: 'Knowing your strengths is vital if you're to present the best possible picture of yourself on application forms, in your CV and at interviews. So you need to ask yourself how well you know your own strengths. Maybe you've heard from your manager about what he or she thinks your strengths are, but appraisal systems often encourage managers to think more about where you need to improve and focus less on where you're already strong.'

## SKILLS AND STRENGTHS

Michelle Bayley adds: 'It's often also easier to identify your skills, your ability to do certain activities well, such as writing or organising, better than your strengths. These are qualities or characteristics you demonstrate, such as determination, enthusiasm or loyalty.'

'The bottom line is that it pays to take responsibility for having a full picture of your strengths, rather than waiting for others to spontaneously tell you what they are.'

For some people, talking about strengths prompts a nagging, critical voice that says: 'You haven't got any strengths', or 'You haven't got any strengths that are worth having'.

Says Bayley: 'Even among the highly talented people I've coached, I've noticed how difficult it often is for them to accept that they have strengths. If you're one of those people, I suggest that you simply notice the critical comment, put it to one side, and allow yourself the chance to get curious about what your strengths are.'

What are your strengths? Here are half a dozen to get you started. See if any of them apply to you. Then see if you can think of any others that do, and add them underneath.

| Strengths | | |
|---|---|---|
| 1. People skills | 2. Creativity | 3. Patience |
| 4. Communication | 5. Composure | 6. Ambition |
| 7. | 8. | 9. |
| 10. | 11. | 12. |

## TELL THE FULL STORY

One way that Craig and Bayley suggest you can start to find your inner Superman or Superwoman is to write a short autobiography. No need to go overboard. Keep it to about 500 or 1000 words. There are a couple of pages at the back of this book that you can use.

*Tip: Think about the whole of your life, not just what's happened in your career. And think about the experiences you've had that have helped make you who you are. What have been the high points? What about the low points? How did you deal with them?*

Here's a half-length example from one of us:

> **My autobiography—Keith Potts**
> - Born 1966.
> - Graduated from Brighton Polytechnic in 1987 with an Honours degree in Computer Science and Statistics.
> - Worked as a software engineer for a defence company.
> - Appointed at Rediffusion Simulation two years later.
> - Responsible for building the instructor station software for industrial full flight simulators for the likes of BA, Delta and UPS.
> - Formed Pinnacle Internet Services Limited with my brother and sister-in-law in 1995.
> - Led the business development of Pinnacle Internet Services as its managing director.
> - Founded Jobsite with my family and Dr Nick Lutte in September 1995.
> - Moved from managing director of Pinnacle to managing director of Jobsite in 1998.
> - Helped drive the growth for Jobsite, which became one of the country's fastest-growing companies.
> - Sold a 49% stake in Jobsite to Manpower Inc in January 2000.
> - The *Sunday Times* Virgin FastTrack ranked Jobsite the sixteenth-fastest growing company in the country in 2001.
> - Sold my entire stock in Pinnacle Internet to Precedent Communications Limited in 2002.

- *Real Business*/Dunn & Bradstreet ranked Jobsite the third-fastest growing UK company in 2003.
- Sold the entire Jobsite stock to Daily Mail and General Trust for £35 million in 2004.
- Became chairman of *www.grassrootscoaching.com*.
- With my family, acquired Norman Carr Safaris Limited, a luxury Zambian safari business.
- Currently managing director of Jobsite UK (Worldwide) Limited.
- I provide the Jobsite organisation with vision and leadership and focus on maintaining Jobsite's success and driving forward new business.
- I'm married, with three children, and enjoy life in Chichester.
- I would like to have more time for my interests, including Formula One, travel, wildlife conservation and reading.

Once you've written your autobiography, read through it and take the time to reflect on any patterns and themes you notice. When you've been at your happiest, what was happening in your life? What does this tell you about what you need to be at your happiest in the future?

And think about how you've dealt with bad times. It can often make you realise you're stronger than you think. All too often we put difficult times behind us, not acknowledging what we've done and who we've been to come through them. What strengths have you shown?

*Taking stock*

As well as writing an autobiography, how about a stock-take of self knowledge? Again, focus on your whole life. Michelle Bayley recommends that you ask six key questions:

1.  What have I done that I'm proud of? Jot down anything from helping a grandparent, to being promoted six months into a job. Don't fall into the trap of only going for the obvious.

2.  What's been my biggest achievement so far? As with what you're proud of, think about what you consider to be an achievement and you know was a stretch for you, not the more obvious things that you think others would be impressed by.

3. When have I felt inspired and/or excited? What were you doing? What kind of people were you with? Remember to think about both work and non-work situations.

4. What motivates me? Is it a challenge, maybe the chance to change things for the better, or the opportunity to help someone or something? What makes you feel like taking action?

5. What's attracted me to my jobs so far? Think back about why you have gone for certain jobs over others. Even where they might not have worked out the way you wanted them to, something led you to them initially.

6. What's been missing in my jobs so far? Your answer to this one will help you define what you need to be happy in future jobs.

## OTHER PATHS TO SELF-KNOWLEDGE

Michelle Bayley lists a number of other ways you can build up a better picture of the kind of person you are. For instance:

■ Think about your current and previous jobs. What strengths have you shown in them? Have you been patient, reliable, determined, self-disciplined, calm under pressure, personable with even the most demanding clients or colleagues? What else?

■ Ask other people. This may sound embarrassing, but hearing others tell you about the strengths they see in you is truly revealing. Says Bayley: 'I ask my coaching clients to choose a mix of friends, family and colleagues or former colleagues and ask each of them to describe that person's top three strengths. And you can offer to do the same for those you ask. We often don't give each other this type of positive feedback, but it carries weight because we know it comes from people who truly know us.'

> *"Hearing others tell you about the strengths they see in you is truly revealing."*

■ Do an online strengths-finder assessment. The book *Now, Discover your Strengths*, by Marcus Buckingham and Donald O Clifton, is based on the idea that we all have signature talents which become our strengths. Buy a copy and you get a password so that you can go to the Strengthsfinder website (www.strengthsfinder.com) and do the assessment.

## WHAT IS YOUR MYERS-BRIGGS PERSONALITY?

One way to find out a lot about yourself is to take a basic psychological profiling test such as the Myers-Briggs Type Indicator (MBTI), which will fit your personality to a given type. This is the kind of test that employers frequently use for their employees, so why not use one yourself to help give yourself the upper hand in your career decisions? The MBTI is particularly useful as it's already widely used in areas such as career counselling and personal development. While the MBTI is technically not meant to be administered other than by qualified practitioners with face-to-face follow up, there are a number of cheap and free tests on the internet (see, for example, *www.personalitypage.com* or *www.humanmetrics.com/cgi-win/JTypes2.asp*) which you can use to work out your personality type in a few minutes.

The MBTI divides people into 16 different personality types, each identified by a four-letter acronym. These range from ISFJs, sometimes called 'Protector Guardians', which make up around 12 to 14% of the population and are primarily concerned with maintaining harmony and caring for people, to ENTJs or 'Fieldmarshals', which make up barely 2% of the population and are natural leaders. As you might expect, certain personality types are more suited to certain types of careers.

### Myers-Briggs and occupations

Thus INFPs, a fairly common type[10] characterised by strong value systems and a desire to help others, may fit naturally into the role of counsellor or teacher. Similarly, ISTJs[11], who are hard workers with good organisational skills, might do well as accountants or computer programmers. Do not be

10. Roughly just over 1 in 10 in the population.
11. Another common type, accounting for around 9% of the population.

put off following a particular career path just because it does not seem suited to your personality. Instead, use your knowledge of your personality type to make sure you can address any shortcomings and increase your chances of career success.

*"Use your knowledge of your personality type to make sure you can address any shortcomings and increase your chances of career success."*

## A QUESTION OF VALUES

With all the above you should be well on your way to building up a pretty complete picture of the person you really are. But one important part of the portrait is still missing: your values. Marianne Craig says: 'Personal values are perhaps the most vital part of the jigsaw of your life in terms of understanding what motivates and fulfils you. We all have values but we are mostly unconscious of them.'

Michelle Bayley adds: 'For the vast majority of us, it's only when we've looked at who we really are and what we really want from life that we can make the right choice about our ideal career.'

'One of the most essential building blocks of who you are is your values. They're the intangible things that are important to us. They're what make us tick. We might have some idea of what they are but we can also be walking around unconscious of some of them too.'

### Trampled values

'For my coaching clients, the crunch often comes when a value is being trampled on. For example, one client didn't realise how much she valued clarity until she worked in a role where her two bosses had conflicting views of what she was there to do. After months of confusion and unhappiness, once she pinpointed what was really bothering her about her job, she took steps to sort things out. And when they still didn't improve, she moved on, recognising that it just wasn't the right organisation for her.'

'Someone else valued co-operation and equality but found herself in a hierarchical, competitive workplace. Again, realising that she wasn't going to be able to live her values allowed her to make a choice and move on to a workplace where her new colleagues did share her values.'

*Work out your values*

 So, if knowing your values is crucial to your happiness, how can you go about identifying them? Bayley proposes three questions which you should ask yourself (or, better still, get someone else to ask you):

1. Who do you admire and what is it that you admire about them? This can be anyone, from a friend, family member or work colleague to someone famous or a historical or fictional character. What we pick up on and admire in others is generally something we value. You might admire someone who's strong or who's upbeat and positive, but feel you're not the same. This doesn't mean that those values aren't important to you, just that you may not have been living them yourself recently, or maybe even for a long time.

2. What annoys you or winds you up? Most of us have things that annoy us, from people who insist on shouting down their mobiles on trains to partners or housemates who leave a trail of mess in their wake. The trick is to flip things over and look for the value that's being quashed. If loud people on mobiles wind you up, chances are you value consideration and thoughtfulness. If you don't like messiness you probably place a high value on organisation and structure.

*"From sitting on a beach watching a beautiful sunrise to being in the middle of a big party, our memories of really great moments hold many clues to our values. Peace, calm and nature could be found in the sunrise moment and connection with others and excitement in the party."*

3.  Think about a peak moment in your life. What was happening? From sitting on a beach watching a beautiful sunrise to being in the middle of a big party, our memories of really great moments hold many clues to our values. Peace, calm and nature could be found in the sunrise moment and connection with others and excitement in the party.

You can carry on until you've got a few dozen values. Once you've thought about what you value, write up your findings and rate each of them on a scale of 1 (low) to 10 (high), according to how much you feel you're living them in your work life at the moment. If you want, you can also rate how much you're experiencing them in the rest of your life. There's no need to agonise over the ratings; they're just a rough guide so you can see which of your values are currently being met and which aren't.

**Applying your values to work**
Next, think about what you can do to help you live your values more fully at work and, again, if you want to, in the rest of your life. For example, if you value learning but feel like you aren't gaining new skills and experience, you could have an action to speak to your manager about training, or getting involved in another area of work.

Ultimately, you might come to the conclusion that there's just too much of a clash between what you value and what matters to your organisation or colleagues, in which case it could be time to move on.

Bayley says: 'You cannot always live all of your values at a full-on ten, but once you know them you know what makes you feel fulfilled. And by acting in line with them, you're taking responsibility for feeling happier about your work and your life as a whole.'

## THE REAL YOU

Now step back and give yourself some time to reflect on all you have got out of the previous exercises. What kinds of things are you good at? What things do you value? What things will make you feel motivated and fulfilled?

Bayley says: 'It might mean setting some time aside in an already busy life, but the more you know about yourself the better you can judge whether a particular job or career possibility is going to give you what you want. This knowledge will enable you to apply for the right jobs rather than just any job that's available.

So now it's time to start thinking about jobs. But where, exactly, do you start?

## TAKE YOUR IDEAS TO THE BANK

A key element in Marianne Craig's Firework Career Coaching approach is a thing called the ideas bank. This is pretty much as it sounds: a place (maybe a folder or ring binder) where you store any ideas about what you might do for work. These can be as specific or tenuous as you like, from 'I want to be a marketing manager for a toy company' to 'I want to work with fun people' or 'I want to work with nature'. The job ideas can be a single word or an entire ad clipped from a paper or printed from an online job board.

*"Job ideas can be a single word or an entire ad clipped from a paper."*

*Tip: It is important that you jot down anything and everything you can think of, and not just in one go … keep your bank going for as long as it takes you to review your situation.*

Note the ideas bank is not intended to provide you with actual job ideas. It is a place for anything and everything you could ever contemplate enjoying, which will give you inspiration and pointers about the kinds of real jobs you might want to pursue. According to Marianne Craig, three ways you could kick start your ideas bank are to:

■ Skim online recruitment websites and job sections of newspapers and magazines, and pull out words, phrases or ads that you feel an affinity for.

■ Think of all the things you have wanted to be throughout your life and find out what they would involve if you went for them now.

■ Look out for jobs that people around you are doing and ask yourself what aspects of those jobs would attract you.

## COULD YOU DO WITH A COACH?

One final thing you might want to think about when entering the planning stage for your career change is whether you might benefit from some professional advice. Career coaching might sound a bit touchy-feely or West Coast American, but, as you can probably tell from what you've read so far in this chapter, coaches spend a lot of time thinking about how best to help you make the right move and have a wealth of experience you can draw on.

Bayley says: "'Why should I work for you?' is practically the statement that all coaching starts with. Coaches work to help you answer the question "Is this role a good match for me?", rather than chasing after jobs with a butterfly net. Typically, we help people who are at a crossroads, people who are sure they want to do something different but don't know where to start. The common thread with them is they're all saying: "I want to get the most out of my work; I am looking for it to be rewarding".

### Could this be you?

Bayley says coaching tends to appeal to professionals in their thirties or older, and has grown in popularity in recent years. How do you know whether it's for you? On her website, Marianne Craig poses three questions for potential clients:

■ Are you successful in your professional life but want to feel more fulfilled?
■ Are you bursting with ideas and want to explore how to take them forward?
■ Do you ask yourself 'Why do I work so hard, but have so little to show for it?'

For many people who opt for coaching, she says, the answer to at least one of these questions tends to be 'yes'. Clearly coaching carries a cost (although Craig offers a free initial coaching consultation), but if you're considering a career change that could affect the rest of your life then the expense could well be worth it.

## WHAT WE'VE LEARNED SO FAR

So, to recap. In the first two chapters of this book you found out why it's time for a rethink of the whole employment process. You learned a bit more about what was working, and not working, in your current job. In this chapter we've gathered together a whole armoury of additional material about you: your strengths, your experience, your values and more.

In the next chapter we are going to build on this knowledge with another, unique profiling tool which will tell you a lot more about yourself as a person and as a worker. It will also help you work out the things *you* should ask potential employers when you go looking for a new job. Sound interesting? Then let's go.

CHAPTER 3:

# Piecing together the ideal job profile

**What you'll get out of this chapter:**
- ■ *Why you should be thinking about getting out of your job if it's not right for you.*
- ■ *A unique profiling tool that will tell you which work environment you'll thrive in.*
- ■ *What your personality profile says about how you live, learn and work.*

AFTER taking the Happy Days test, we sincerely hope you've confirmed that you're leading a happy, balanced life. If so, brilliant! You can scrap reading the rest of this book and skip to work with joy in your heart. (Better still, put this book away somewhere carefully for future reference ... after all, you never know ... or hand it over to someone you know who might not be having such a good time at work.) However, if your work life is affecting your home life or, if one or several things about your job are getting you down, then don't despair.

The most important thing to realise is that whilst inaction is easier, if you're unhappy only you have the ultimate power to change it and there are some simple ways to do this, as we will see. And you know what else? If you're not having a good time at work then you're definitely not alone.

*"If you're not having a good time at work then you're definitely not alone."*

## UNHAPPY@WORK

As we've seen, a significant proportion of workers in the United Kingdom are not happy with their jobs. That equates to millions of employees. Why the long faces?

In a study by a human resources consultancy called Chiumento[12], where only a quarter of respondents said they were very happy in their jobs and one in five of those polled were unhappy, the main factors causing all our unhappiness at work were listed as follows. Tick how many apply to you:

- ■ Lack of communication from bosses.
- ■ Uncompetitive salary.
- ■ No recognition for achievements.
- ■ Poor boss or line manager.
- ■ Few options for personal development.
- ■ Ideas being ignored.
- ■ Lack of opportunities for good performers.
- ■ Lack of benefits.

In contrast, the eight top things that were said to contribute to our happiness at work were the following. How many do you recognise?

- ■ Friendly, supportive colleagues.
- ■ Enjoyable work.
- ■ A good boss or line manager.
- ■ A good work-life balance.
- ■ Varied work.
- ■ Belief that we are doing something worthwhile.
- ■ Feeling that what we do makes a difference.
- ■ Being part of a successful team.

Factors such as having a good boss or lack of benefits are ones which we would instinctively recognise as improving, or detracting from, our enjoyment of work. Work that is stimulating and rewarding and for which you're appreciated and supported is likely to make you happier than a job where your role is unclear and there is little prospect of rewards, recognition and improvement. Is it really worth all this research to come up with stuff that we already know? Well, hang on, because it might be … if we take the science a little further.

12. From *Personnel Today*, 8 January, 2007: 'Friendly colleagues rather than money make people happy at work'. The Chiumento Happiness Index covered 1,060 UK employees.

## A NEW WAY OF LOOKING AT WORKERS

It goes without saying that the kinds of rankings produced by surveys such as the Chiumento one only give us a view of the 'average' worker. But no one is average. Each of us has different priorities, likes and dislikes.

*"Each of us has different priorities, likes and dislikes."*

For you, the top priority in a job might be to make wads of cash. But it might equally be to spend more time with your family. Or gain recognition from your peers. Or whatever. It is very unlikely to be the same thing as what motivates the next person. And not only that: it's also likely to change over time. A motivated 20-something might well be happy to put in the hours in order to get a foothold on the corporate ladder, but when they reach 40 they may start to feel it's more important to spend time with their family.

## BEYOND THE DATA

So how do you get beyond the raw data to develop a better understanding of what motivates you, at different times in your life, and how that might help you improve your working experience? In 2005, on its tenth anniversary, the online recruitment website Jobsite decided to look in detail at how a specific range of jobs might suit people with a specific range of personalities. Consultant Rafe Offer says: 'We realised that different people want different things from their work life, will need different management and will be attracted by completely different things.

'We also realised that if the individual doesn't match the company culture, it's a lose-lose situation for both parties.'

Jobsite carried out focus group discussions with job hunters, surveyed 5000 people and finally teamed up with an expert called Dr Paul Morgan, author of *Managing Yourself: Mastering Your Emotional Intelligence*, to create a set of distinct profiles that define employees. The Jobsite Personal Profiles follow a segmentation scheme that is backed by half a century of academic research and is already used in putting together top sports teams. It was even instrumental in helping to overcome apartheid in South Africa.

## THE DEEPER WORLD OF WORKERS' VIEWS

'The Jobsite framework goes beneath the surface descriptions of the different work types, such as technical, managerial or entrepreneurial, and identifies the deeper world of workers' views,' explains Offer, who helped lead the development work on the profiles. 'It recognises that people's values and motivational drivers are fluid and will change according to life circumstances.

'It also recognises that you can't separate work and life, so it's a holistic approach. It changed everything for Jobsite: its own recruitment, how it trains and manages staff, its website and, most importantly, its understanding of job hunters.' Great! So how does it work, then?

## THE JOBSITE PERSONAL PROFILE TYPES

According to the test, there are five major types of worker, as defined by the way they live their lives and their priorities for life and work. Look through the following and decide which description fits you best. (And if you have problems gauging exactly which category you fall into, you can find out in just eight minutes online at *www.jobsite.co.uk/personalprofile*.)

*"There are five major types of worker, as defined by the way they live their lives and their priorities for life and work."*

### Balancers

**Balancers** seek flexibility at work. If you're a balancer you will be keen to carefully and passionately manage your time to get the most out of your life. You will prefer a job that you enjoy but which still allows you to balance a career with other priorities. You appreciate this flexibility in all areas of your work, your interactions with friends and family, and your life in general.

*"If you're a balancer you will be keen to carefully and passionately manage your time to get the most out of your life."*

The best type of organisation for you is one where people are treated as the most valuable asset and you can work in an atmosphere of informality, friendliness and democracy. Work is not the be-all and end-all, but a means to an end.

*Balancer characteristics*
- Manages time to get the most out of life.
- Wants an interesting job but has other priorities.
- Appreciates flexibility at work.
- Enjoys informality, friendliness and democracy.

### Believers

A **believer** lives in a world with almost infinite possibilities. You believe people should be pursuing their passions and not be caught up by what others say they should desire.

Your entire life involves continuously having new experiences and learning from them. It is the challenge, the risk, the prospect of what you can achieve that drives you, rather than simply making money, for instance.

You are a self-motivated individual driven by your passion and so you need a job and an environment with loose boundaries and the maximum freedom.

(As an aside, this 'anything is possible' attitude of believers makes them quite likely to become entrepreneurs. One of us is a typical believer … and a serial entrepreneur. We haven't put Virgin boss Richard Branson through the profile test to see what type he is, but … well, what do you think?)

*Believer characteristics*
- Loves to work.
- Thinks the world has infinite possibilities.
- Believes people should pursue their passions.
- Able to take risks.
- Life involves learning from new experiences.

## Contenders

As a **contender,** you're likely to think that at times it's necessary for work to come before the family, with the knowledge that the family will benefit in the long run from your success. You believe that in a world of opportunities only the strongest survive. So to guarantee your survival you make things happen. You are able to set goals and to focus on achieving them, not afraid to make difficult decisions or take risks. The last thing you want is a dead-end job. You want to move on up and be rewarded for your efforts and ability.

### Contender characteristics

- Career-minded.
- Puts work before family.
- Believes only the strongest survive.
- Unafraid of tough decisions or risks.
- Makes things happen—but can be ruthless.

## Supporters

As a **supporter**, your focus is not so much on yourself but on your family or dependants. They always come before work and you see your job very much as something that has to fit in with your life (and that of your dependants) rather than the other way around. This means you will usually want a job where you can turn up, do a good day's work and then go home with no added pressure. You don't want the extra responsibility of having to make decisions; you would rather someone else in authority told you what to do, and how well to do it.

You believe in rules and structures in life, particularly in the workplace, to help make sure that everyone knows what they need to do. Your bosses are likely to see you as a trustworthy safe pair of hands.

### Supporter characteristics

- Family oriented, puts home life before work.
- Doesn't want responsibility or decision-making power.
- Likes rules and structures at work.
- Dependable.

**Survivors**

**Survivors** have a strong focus on getting what they want and getting it quickly. You believe in survival of the fittest and the law of the jungle, where each person needs to do what it takes to thrive. You're not scared of physical challenges or taking risks. When you make a decision, you don't waste time on lengthy evaluations or complex calculations. You do it on instinct, gut feeling. And when it comes to work, you're not after a career, just a wage that will allow you to keep your head above water and obtain the things that you want from life. You don't mind a hard day's work for a fair day's pay.

*Survivor characteristics*
- Strong.
- Focused.
- Believes in survival of the fittest.
- Unafraid of physical challenges or risks.
- Not looking for a career, just a wage.

What does your profile say about you and your social, personal and work preferences? Read on to find out[13].

## THE BALANCER

### Balancer social values
*Family*
Some people spend all their time at work and others prefer to put the family first, but you believe that there can, and should, be a balance between work, home and other aspects of your life. You're a great advocate of equality and within your family you're committed to members being equal. There is an emphasis on joint participation and collaboration on interests and pursuits.

*Community*
You support the notion that people actively create their own communities. Here, like-minded people seek each other out and come together. Many forms

---

13. You'll notice that some of the points we provide are the same from one personality type to another. This is because there are areas of overlap between the different personalities. In the same way, if you have difficulty deciding whether you belong to one profile or another, it might be that you're borderline between the two, and may tend to either depending on your circumstances.

of community can be created. These communities often have an emphasis on social welfare and mutual support, with all members having equal standing. The members co-create their jointly-held values and pursue group harmony.

### Life view

For you, everything works best when people carefully manage their time so as to get the most out of their whole lives. Through this successful management you believe that life has the potential to be truly harmonious. It may be idealistic, but you view the world as a 'single family' and that all people are created equal and are fundamentally caring and decent. Our responsibilities stretch beyond humankind however, with the need to take care of the natural world of animals and plants.

## Balancer personal values

### Personal preferences

You're committed to being inclusive and democratic. You are a supporter of human rights and will be participative in activities supporting those rights. This mindset extends to working for the benefit of nature and the world as a whole.

Only in the eyes of our mum do we tend to be perfect. In reality, there are usually a few things we're not so good at. For you, sometimes you may be susceptible to being influenced by peer pressure and at times may not take things to their ultimate conclusion. Being such a good people-person, you're also disinclined to work alone, which may restrict or limit you.

### Learning preferences

Everyone has a preferred way of learning and for you it's while working 'alongside' the other learners. You enjoy group tasks and the ability to help others and be helped. You're not one for the stand-at-the-front-of-class-and-dictate approach to teaching, you much prefer tutors to 'work as a partner with you'; often in a role that resembles a coach/mentor rather than a classroom tutor. You are happy to explore your feelings in learning environments.

> *"You enjoy group tasks and the ability to help others and be helped."*

*Tip: You find yourself drawn towards state-of-the-art learning methods and learning technologies. Be happy to accept teaching, monitoring and coaching if it helps you to achieve more.*

### Decision-making preferences

You firmly believe that decisions should be made by the appropriate team or group. This will be achieved through discussion where feelings are valued as much as facts. You desire collaborative decisions where reaching consensus is deemed very important. The approach is distinctly democratic.

### Motivational preferences

People's motivations can vary considerably. You are motivated by a desire to have a balance between your life and your work in its entirety. This is why you appreciate flexibility in your life, work and interactions. You respond well to being treated in a friendly and humane way and are attracted to opportunities to freely interact with others. Teamwork is important to you and so you strive to maintain a group cohesion and welcome the use of team-based incentives.

In terms of getting something back, you appreciate it, as it's only fair, when consistent, dependable and long-term service is recognised and rewarded.

## Balancer work values

### Job type

You prefer a job structure which allows and encourages social interaction. The focus should be on collaboration amongst colleagues rather than competition between them. The job should allow lateral movement and team working to help the organisation to achieve its objectives. There should be minimum emphasis on hierarchical job roles. Instead, people should count. It's important though that your job should not detach you from your community.

### Preferred communication style

For you the freedom to communicate is essential. This is not only with task-related interactions; you relish the scope to explore emotions. You are comfortable with ambiguous language, which may include the use of anecdotes and stories. You're most comfortable with informality and friendliness in communications, where the focus is more upon communication between 'equals' than up and down a hierarchy.

*"You're most comfortable with informality and friendliness in communications."*

*Preferred organisational environment*
If you're going to be happy in your job, you need to find a company that suits the way you like to work. For you, it's in organisations where people are treated as the most valuable asset. You want an environment where informality and friendliness are the norm, rather than an emphasis on roles and impersonal interactions. For you to thrive, the structure should be distinctly non-authoritarian and should not encourage competitiveness. You want an organisation where consensus and feelings may be valued more highly than tasks and outcomes.

## THE BELIEVER

### Believer social values
*Family*
Some people have great difficulty balancing their work life and family, often resorting to choosing one over the other. Not you. You can see that at times your career will come first and at others, it will be your family. All permutations and combinations are open to you; you don't feel bound by one or another. You also accept that the roles of family members may shift, just as your own do, and that each member has remarkable potential.

*Tip: You're a great advocate of equality and within your family you're committed to members being equal. So look for activities where there is an emphasis on joint participation and collaboration on interests and pursuits.*

*Community*
You believe that it is possible to have many forms of community. You may wish to be part of some communities but only if it excites you and fires your passions. Conversely, you may step outside of communities and do what serves your personal – and individual – passions. You chose.

*Life view*
In your opinion, the world has almost infinite possibilities. It offers each person many ways to live and express him/her self. You believe people should be pursuing their passions and not be caught up by what others say they should desire. You feel there are endless ways people can live their lives and believe

*"You believe people should be pursuing their passions"*

life has the capacity to be harmonious and beautiful. Ultimately, people should live fully and responsibly.

## Believer personal values

### Personal preferences

On the plus side, you have a strong and continuous desire to keep learning, with an unwavering commitment to self-development. You are able to find what excites you and then require no external incentives to work hard. You have the capacity to synthesise and find new ways of being.

Sometimes you may become impatient with others who do not think in your way. You may be perceived as unhelpful or uncooperative as you tend to do your own thing. This can give the perception that you're not a non-team player as you won't 'dance to other people's tunes.'

*"Sometimes you may become impatient with others who do not think in your way."*

### Learning preferences

Everyone has a preferred way of learning. For you, your entire life involves continuously having new experiences and learning from them. You have the capacity to learn from others; whether they be formal teachers, facilitators, coaches or role models. You will also use every appropriate technology to assist you in your learning. Once you are passionate about a subject you will absorb information in any way that suits you. For you to live is to learn and learning is an end in itself.

### Decision making preferences

You have a confident approach to decision making, whereby you make decisions on the basis of what excites and energises you and you don't fear the consequences of the choices you make. That's not to say you're reckless, rather you're confident in your ability to live with those consequences. You are equally at home with using analytical tools to make a decision or simply to trust your instincts. You may or may not consult with other people but whatever the circumstances the decision will be your responsibility. You love to take on new challenges and respond flexibly to the situation.

### Motivational preferences

You're a self-motivated individual driven by your passion for a subject or project. When you get passionate about a work-based project there is no stopping you – you just get on with it, needing no encouragement or incentives from others. Indeed, if someone attempts to directly motivate you it's more likely to have the reverse effect. You much prefer an open, flexible, environment where you're free to get on with things without interference.

## Believer work values
### Job type
You prefer a job structure that has loose boundaries and allows you the maximum freedom. You welcome the option of collaborative synergies that you may or may not utilise, rather than pre-determined groups. However as you may choose to do things alone, a structure open enough to cope with the unpredictability of your approach is required.

### Preferred communication style
As you have a tremendous capacity to process information, you're able to absorb it from a variety of sources in a variety of ways. Personally, you want the freedom to communicate with who you want and at whatever time suits you. Consequently, you resent any attempt by others to control and direct the flow of information. For you, the more open and flexible the better.

*"Personally, you want the freedom to communicate with who you want and at whatever time suits you."*

### Preferred organisational environment
You work best in organisations where boundaries are flexible and fluid. Ideally, there should be little or no emphasis on hierarchies and the greater the opportunities for self-determinism and autonomy the more you like it.

The kind of organisation that interests you most is one that has the people and facilities to allow maximum scope for personal development. If it's committed to learning, continuous improvement and excellence it's going to be more attractive to you. An organisation structure that limits your freedom of thought and action is likely to cause you to leave.

## THE CONTENDER

### Contender social values

*Family*

There are times in your life when the worlds of work and home life collide and you have to make a choice of which must come first. As you tend to have a focus on upward mobility, you're likely to believe that at times it's necessary for work to come before the family. Consequently, this may require the sacrifice of family concerns in order to advance your career. For example, you may have to work very long hours and your family must accept that this may happen sometimes. However, by you becoming more successful your family can reap the rewards.

*Community*

The notion of community is not really that important to you. You do socialise with people but it tends to be those who share your ambitions or motivations. However, you're not really a group person so you maintain your distance and your individuality. You also don't have a problem with disrupting a social group or community if your actions will enable you to make some progress.

On a larger scale, you find a focus on community values potentially suffocating and feel there is little scope for stable communities in a fast-changing world.

*Life view*

In your opinion, the world works best when each individual pursues their own self-interest. When people can enjoy individual success they will unleash all their creativity and energy. In a world of possibilities and opportunities, the strongest thrive. You think people who achieve are admirable and make good role models.

*"You think people who achieve are admirable and make good role models."*

### Contender personal values

*Personal preferences*

You are a person who makes things happen. You set goals and focus upon achieving them. You can identify opportunities and then energetically take action. Rather handily, when required you are also pretty good at operating politically. But no-one could accuse you of being afraid of hard work – you'll even work towards team goals as long as your own efforts will be recognised and rewarded.

The downside of all this is unfortunately others may perceive you as a little selfish. As you focus so intently on the task, you may have a tendency to be insensitive to the needs and feelings of others around you. In certain environments you will appear 'too political' or overly and unnecessarily competitive.

### Learning preferences

For you, learning tends to be a means to an end. And the end will tend to be success. You have a lot of energy for learning. You are constantly looking for information or ideas that will give you that all-important edge. You prefer learning objectives to be set and then to have the opportunity to identify and try out potential solutions. You find yourself drawn towards state of the art learning methods and learning technologies and will happily accept teaching, monitoring and coaching if it helps you to achieve more.

> *"Your decisions will not be limited to conservative options as you are willing to take risks."*

### Decision-making preferences

Some people have difficulty making decisions, but not you, especially when you can decide and then take action. Your decisions tend to focus on how to achieve a goal or outcome. When making a decision you are more comfortable with a range of options to choose from. You like to test the options and consult experts if appropriate. Your decisions will not be limited to conservative options as you are willing to take risks.

### Motivational preferences

People tend to be motivated by different things. Your motivation comes from significant and visible improvements in your status and visible, clear performance targets. You like to know how well you're doing so you prefer it when you get to monitor your own progress. You like the opportunity to show your capabilities to others and you will work within a team context as long as objectives are clear and your personal contributions can be recognised.

## Contender work values

*Job type*
The best job for you is one where your rewards are explicitly linked to your effort and ability. The focus for you is on the job being part of a career path rather than a more day to day job. You're at your most comfortable in a competitive, demanding environment where the job provides scope for you to solve problems and use your own creativity and talents.

*Preferred communication style*
Good communication is essential for everyone, but different people have different preferences for the way it's done. You prefer communications to be task-related, with all key objectives, actions and agreements documented.

*Tip: You like to keep up to date with all the latest business phrases and this should be reflected in communication. The emphasis should be on being positive, up beat and with a can-do attitude. Look out for opportunities to communicate your ability and efforts, be it in formal presentations, the way you dress, the car you drive, or through your confident demeanour.*

*Preferred organisational environment*
If you're going to be happy in your job, you need to find a company that suits the way you like to work. You work best in an organisation where your efforts can be recognised and rewarded. You prefer a hierarchical, performance-based business, with a meritocratic environment. You don't want to languish in a dead-end job, so you want to see evidence of employees starting at the bottom and working their way to the top. The structure is one that should enable rapid movement and greater mobility.

*"You don't want to languish in a dead-end job, so you want to see evidence of employees starting at the bottom and working their way to the top."*

The best place to work is one where everyone is subject to tough, demanding targets. They should be encouraged to come up with new ways of doing things.

## THE SUPPORTER

### Supporter social values
*Family*
Your family is very important to you and like many of us, you believe it should always come before work. For you, the role of the family is to teach values, morals and the correct way to behave. You feel more comfortable and at ease when you're in your own home and you live for your weekends and holidays when you can get away from work and spend time with your family.

*Community*
You believe that a community works best when people have clear roles and status levels. When everyone knows how they fit in to the community and what their position is. As a good member of the community you don't want to cause trouble or rock the boat. You know your place and believe most people are part of a stable quiet majority.

> *"You believe that a community works best when people have clear roles and status levels."*

*Life view*
Everything works better when it's really clear who does what, who's in charge and what rules we have to follow. Otherwise there is chaos when people mess things up by just doing what they want. People should have some self-discipline and it's only right they should be punished if they break the rules. And likewise, if you do what's expected of you, then you should be rewarded appropriately.

People tend not to be perfect, so the best thing to do is obey the law or the rules and do what you're told by the people in authority. The emphasis should be on doing your duty and what is expected.

### Supporter personal values
*Personal preferences*
You're at your happiest when you know your place and can get on with working to the rules that have been laid down. The people around you, including your boss, view you as a 'safe pair of hands' - someone who they can depend upon. You have no difficulty following instructions and believe that offering a dependable service is important. When people think of you, they think 'reliable' – it's like your trademark!

It's likely you're not a big fan of change and you're likely to resist it. At times you might come across as a bit judgemental, as you 'stick to your guns' when defending the 'right way' to do something. You also tend not to want to take risks and sometimes people might see this as being inflexible.

### Learning preferences

You prefer to be taught by a well-organised and accepted authority on the subject. You work best if the instructions they give you are spelled out clearly and precisely define the standards you're expected to reach. If that all happens and you or someone else still gets it wrong, you've no problem with errors being punished appropriately.

### Decision-making preferences

Not everyone is great at decision-making, but you'll be happy to make decisions if you have first been shown exactly how a decision should be made. Once rules for decision-making have been established you will apply them rigorously and without ambiguity. If there is any ambiguity and it's not clear, you expect someone in authority to make the appropriate decision. You'll then carry out any actions that are expected of you.

### Motivational preferences

You have a strong desire to make sure the things you do are done to an acceptable level. You don't want to be seen to not be doing something well enough. Especially as most of the time these levels are set by people with seniority, people like your boss. And if need be, you're willing to make sacrifices as long as they're reasonable.

> *"You have a strong desire to make sure the things you do are done to an acceptable level."*

In terms of getting something back, you appreciate it when consistent, dependable and long-term service is recognised and rewarded.

## Supporter work values

### Job type

You like to be in a place where you're given a clearly defined job structure. Where you can turn up to work, get a good day's work done and then go home. No vagueness, no waffle. You expect yourself and your colleagues to follow the correct procedures and work orders and when they're not followed, you can expect to get into trouble.

The more precisely defined your job is, the more you like it. You don't like changes in your job. Instead you prefer a job that is secure, stable and unchanging. You like to focus on doing your job correctly and prefer to leave others to do likewise.

As for loyalty, it's important to you to be a loyal employee and in return you expect to be treated with respect.

### Preferred communication style
Within an organisation you prefer it if senior people clearly describe all the appropriate rules, processes and regulations. The greater the precision, the more comfortable you are with the communication. The message underpinning communication should always focus upon doing your duty and on reliability.

The greater the formality, clarity and brevity, the more you like it. The last thing you want is someone spouting jargon and gobbledegook. You'd rather a plain speaking, more conservative language.

### Preferred organisational environment
You work best in organisations with a formal and recognisable hierarchy. It's important to you to be told exactly where you fit within that hierarchy, including knowing whom you report to and who reports to you. You're also going to want to know all the procedures and rules that apply to your job.

> *"You work best in organisations with a formal and recognisable hierarchy."*

For the most part, you believe that rewards go to people for delivering to standards and for seniority. For you, by delivering to standards you can demonstrate your worthiness within the organisation.

*Tip: For your comfort and peace of mind, where possible try to work for an organisation that is predictable and risks are low to zero.*

## THE SURVIVOR

### Survivor social values
*Family*

You have a strong belief in the tradition of family. However, you do tend to expect to get things your own way and to have the family comply with your wishes. You have a tendency to have an 'us against the world' mentality, which can be seen in how the family stick together and protect one another.

*Community*

You're not really one for the notion of community; it's a bit too 'touchy-feely' for you. You'd rather focus on getting what you want and getting it quickly. When groups or communities get in your way you're not averse to trying to intimidate others to get what you want. Rather than social concerns you believe the strongest individual should rule. Communities just frustrate you and get in the way of you doing your own thing.

> *"You're not really one for the notion of community; it's a bit too 'touchy-feely' for you."*

*Life view*

From your perspective, the world is an uncaring and a dangerous place. It is a tough jungle environment where the main rule is survival of the fittest. Each person has to do whatever it takes to survive and to thrive. When you rely on people you make yourself vulnerable to attack. Human nature is brutal, so you must be willing to humiliate others before they get you.

### Survivor personal values
*Personal preferences*

Your strengths are evident in your willingness to take physical challenges and risks. If times become difficult or dangerous, you can tough it out. You don't mind doing a hard day's work for a fair day's pay, either. And you certainly wouldn't hesitate to fight your corner.

You're not a big fan of collaborating with others and if it gets results you do tend to bully people. You can be perceived as self-centred and dismissive of authority, unless it's tough. You probably wouldn't be classed as a people person as your approach may scare people.

### Learning preferences

Everyone has a preferred way of learning. For you learning should have immediate pay off. You prefer it to be kept simple and straightforward and for feedback to be immediate. You respect teachers that are firm, but you're not really interested in long-term learning plans or overly complex subjects.

### Decision-making preferences

The process of who makes decisions is quite simple for you. If you're the most powerful person you make the decisions. You don't waste time doing complicated calculations, you do it on instinct, on gut feeling.

Tip: Don't bother sleeping on decisions. Make them straight away, so you can get stuck into things. And if someone is more powerful than you then let them make the decision.

### Motivational preferences

Some people rely on others to motivate them. Not you, you are motivated by your own impulses. What you feel like or desire is what eggs you on into action. You will set very immediate goals and do things if you think they are challenging or daring. You also like showing people how brave and tough you can be.

> "What you feel like or desire is what eggs you on into action."

## Survivor work values

### Job type

Complicated job structures don't interest you. Instead you prefer simple, easy-to-follow tasks. You don't mind if the work is physically demanding nor will you chicken out if the work is hard. All you want is a wage, preferably a daily or weekly one at that. It'd be a foolish person who tries to get you to do paperwork. You'd much rather get your hands dirty with a manual job. All this focus on team work and touchy-feely management drives you crazy.

Give you a boss who's strong and direct and will keep you in line, any day of the week.

### Preferred communication style

You want people senior to you to be no nonsense and very direct. Forget the flowery language or jargon. In fact, you are more comfortable with the occasional swear word and aggressiveness. Given a choice you prefer face to face communication rather than memos or emails.

### Preferred organisational environment

If you're going to be happy in your job, you need to find a company that suits the way you like to work. You prefer an organisation where the most powerful and dominant people are at the top. You can respect that way of operating. You also believe people should have physically challenging jobs and those who can't cut it should be kicked out immediately. You'd rather the environment be one which supports courage, strength and prowess. The less complicated the better.

## WHAT PROFILE DO YOU FIT INTO?

More than 110,000 Jobsite Personal Profile tests have been completed to date, giving Jobsite a pretty accurate picture of the different proportions of each type of worker in the overall population.

Survivors are by far the least common type, making up less than 1% of the population at any point in time.

Around half the population, it turns out, is made up of balancers[14]. Just over a fifth of the population are contenders, while believers and supporters make up around 17 and 12% of the total, respectively. If you have worked out which category you fit into, you may also have tried to work out which types of jobs would be suited to each category. A survivor, for example, might be suited to a hands-on, active job such as being a fire fighter.

---

14. Or, at least, around half the people who have taken the test are balancers. However, these are probably the most likely people to take such a test because they're keen to find out more about themselves.

A supporter might like the structure and stability of working as an administrator. A contender might aspire to be a managing director. But the point about these definitions is not so much to identify what type of job you might end up doing, but what characteristics of a particular job will make it a good fit with your personality. After all, in virtually any form of employment, in any sector, there is likely to be a requirement for survivors, supporters, balancers, believers and contenders.

*"In virtually any form of employment, in any sector, there is likely to be a requirement for survivors, supporters, balancers, believers and contenders."*

There are many reasons why we might not like a job, and they might not be obvious ones. It might just be that feeling of 'something is not right'. Being able to work out what kind of worker profile you have, and how it measures up against your job, might help you work out where the problem lies.

### Time and change

Also, you have to bear in mind that you may well move from one category to another as you move through life. Let's take a hypothetical example. A person joins the employment pool in their late teens. At that point, their interests are in going out, having fun, enjoying themselves and earning enough to be able to afford all this. They are not really too fussed about the kind of work they do, as long as it pays the bills; a typical survivor. Some years pass, and work becomes more centre-stage. Our employee is now willing to make sacrifices for their career.

### Shifting the balance

Instead of nights out, it's nights in, in the office, because they believe this will get them ahead. They have become a contender. But this does not last forever. With the arrival of a family, for example, they may feel it's time to re-focus on life and seek a more flexible working arrangement, typical of a balancer. Later on, they may even shift the focus more fully onto their family, handing back part of the responsibility they have achieved at work so they spend more time with their loved ones: a classic supporter profile.

## WHERE WE ARE NOW

Knowing which of these categories you fit into at any given point in your life can be an important step in working out whether your job is right for you. In helping you avoid that feeling of being a square peg in a round hole. In making you feel good about working, and consequently working well. In short, in becoming truly happy at work. Now it's time to stop looking inwards and start looking outwards at your current job, and ask: can it be improved? Or should I really move on? It's time for action. Are you ready?

CHAPTER 4:

# Should I stay or should I go?

**What you'll get out of this chapter:**

- ◾ *Six sure-fire suggestions to improve communication with your current employer.*
- ◾ *The six best moments to talk about a pay rise.*
- ◾ *Half a dozen ways to get more money out of your current employer even if they won't give you a pay rise.*

When we find gainful employment we are conditioned to view it as something precious, not to be given up lightly. And then there is the fear of a switch not going as planned. Whether or not you're in it for the money, there is something tremendously reassuring about the monthly pay cheque. We rely on it to pay our bills, mortgages and living expenses, even if there might not be much left over by the time the next pay day comes around. We may also rely on our employer for a pension, car, private medical insurance, gym membership and more.

# We may be happy to give up a job; but are we prepared to sacrifice the security of the pay cheque and employment package, even for a short while?

Well, the answer may not be as clear-cut as you think, as we will see later on in this chapter. But for now, let's accept that if you're going to find a better job, perhaps the simplest place to start is with the devil you know: your existing employer.

*"If you're going to find a better job, perhaps the simplest place to start is with the devil you know: your existing employer."*

## WHAT DON'T YOU LIKE AT WORK?

Improving your current lot without moving is a great idea, if you can manage it. It is probably easiest where your job is already close to perfect (for example, if you get high or medium scores in the Happy Days test), so that your employer has to make only a few adjustments to be assured of your loyalty. It is very possible they will accommodate your wishes. Since 7 out of 10 employers believe that when an employee leaves it has a negative effect on business performance[15], it's in their interests to keep you on. Just be careful that the improvements you're pushing for are realistic. If your company's profits are down, asking for a £10k pay rise isn't going to happen and you might damage your relatonship with your boss. So let's take a look at why things aren't so great with your work right now, and what can be done about them.

### Workplace niggles
According to the Chartered Institute of Personnel and Development, the main workplace gripes are:
- Lack of communication from bosses.
- Uncompetitive salary.
- No recognition for achievements.
- Poor boss or line manager.
- Few options for personal development.
- Ideas being ignored.
- Lack of opportunities for good performers.
- Lack of benefits.

Now let's take each in turn and see what we can do about it.

---

15. From the 2007 annual survey report on recruitment, retention and turnover from the Chartered Institute of Personnel and Development.

*Get your bosses to talk to you*
Whether it's general information on whether the company is doing well enough to guarantee you a bonus this year, or direct feedback on why you're being passed over for promotion, lack of communication from your superiors is a workplace problem for many of us ... but one that many of us can also remedy without too much trouble. However, it's important to remember that communication is a two-way process, so you have to do your bit, too.

# Most employers recognise the need to communicate effectively and if they don't then it's not usually intentional.

*Tip: If you've got a communication problem, the first thing to do is ... communicate! Raise the issue with your boss or bosses.*

What to do if your employer doesn't seem to recognise the problem? Here are six simple suggestions:

- If you don't have a regular forum for communication, such as a weekly team meeting, then request it from your boss — and get them to make it a priority.

- If you do have such events but you don't think you're getting the information you need out of them, then see if it would be possible to add extra items to the agenda which will cover the points you need to know about.

- Look out for opportunities to talk informally with your superiors and team-mates. Attending leaving dos or after-hours get-togethers might not always be easy if you have a busy social schedule or a family to look after, but they could repay the effort in terms of giving you a chance to corner your boss.

*"Look out for opportunities to talk informally with your superiors and team-mates."*

■ Similarly, watch out for water-cooler moments and other work-time opportunities for information communication. If your boss is an early bird or stays late then it might be worth changing your own timetable once in a while so you coincide at times when it might be easier to chat.

■ If you tend to work away from your boss then it's easy to miss out on important day-to-day contact time. Ask your IT department whether they can give you tools such as an instant messenger system or a smart-phone to help you keep in touch.

■ Beyond your own boss, use staff suggestions schemes and internal communications programmes to request more information from your employer. If there isn't a staff suggestions scheme then why not suggest one?

### Making more money

It's probably fair to say that none of us would mind getting paid a bit more for what we do. At the same time, though, it's a pretty gutsy (or foolhardy) employee who will just stride in to see their boss and demand a pay rise out of the blue. Getting more money out of your employer is often at least partially down to factors which may be beyond your control, such as whether the business has had a good year.

# If the amount you're getting paid is really getting you down, then ideally you need to create an excuse to have a conversation about it.

This could happen if you get another job offer, for example, but you do not necessarily need to have another potential employer waiting in the wings in order to talk to your boss about cash.

Occasions which you could use to discuss your pay include:
- Whenever you have a formal or informal review.

- If you're asked to take on extra work, for example due to a change in role or to cover for maternity leave.

- If there are changes in your colleagues' circumstances, such as a review of job responsibilities.

- At the end of year or when business budgets or targets are being announced.

- If work imposes an additional burden on you, for instance by asking you to relocate or work unreasonable hours.

- Occasionally, if there are changes in the wider economy or your personal circumstances that might warrant a pay discussion. For example: 'My mortgage payments have gone up so much lately that I simply can't afford to live off my salary any longer. Is there anything the company can do?'

*Six ways to get more money without a pay rise*
Of course, you can ask for a pay rise until you're blue in the face … but that doesn't mean you will get one. However, if you have tried for an increase and it's clear that you won't get one (for instance, because the company is having to make cutbacks), don't despair. Here are six ways in which you can get more money from your employer *without getting a pay rise*.

- Increase your pension contributions and ask your employer to match them. Many employers will be happy to do this because there are tax advantages in it for them.

- Find out if you have a say in where your pension money gets invested. You might be able to switch funds and get a better rate of return.

- If you're generally happy with your employer, help them to find more employees. Many companies have rewards schemes for employee referrals.

- Ask your employer to pay for job-related training. Every course you take increases your value as an employee and most employers will be happy to make the investment.

- Check to see if you could be rewarded in other ways than a pay rise, for instance by getting share options, private healthcare or a company car. Look around you to see what others are benefiting from at your level.

- Look to get rewarded for providing extra value for your employer. For example, see if you could be paid a bonus for bringing in new business or taking on additional duties. Dropping a hint prior to a contract signup is a good way of broaching this subject.

### Get more recognition for what you do

You work your backside off for your company then some boss/colleague/outside consultant gets all the credit for your hard work. Sound familiar? Of course it does. Who hasn't felt hard-done by when it comes to being praised? And if you're under 30, you're likely to feel it even more acutely. A US poll by a company called Leadership IQ found that Generation Y workers — those aged between 21 and 30 — were much more likely than older ones to be motivated by recognition, and 6 out of 10 said they weren't getting it[16].

Unfortunately, getting your employer to say 'thank you' more often, and mean it, is easier said than done. Providing recognition is something some individuals, and companies, are just good at … and others aren't. But don't let that put you off trying to solve the situation. Here are a few pointers on what you can do:

- Try to start a praise culture yourself, by saying thanks as often as possible to colleagues and superiors.

- Look at what you currently do and see if there are any changes you could make to deserve praise more often, for instance by offering to help out more frequently.

- Sell yourself and your successes. Not everyone is a born self-publicist, of course, but if you're proud of your achievements at work then there is no harm in sharing your elation. Many people do this quite skilfully without giving the impression that they're big-headed.

16. See *Want to motivate Generation Y? Try praise, attention*, Reuters, 29 November, 2007.

*Ditch your boss*

Working for someone you don't get on with is a real nightmare, not least because you're liable to feel that you have no option than to get out of your job, no matter how you feel about the company you work for. In actual fact, though, many companies are likely to be a lot more understanding of your situation than you might expect, not least because Human Resources professionals recognise that it's not always easy to put together teams that click.

*Tip: If you're having problems with your boss, don't be afraid of biting the bullet and talking to your Human Resources department, or your boss's boss, about the problem. They may well propose measures that make it easier for you and your manager to get on, but if that doesn't work, and you're in the least bit good at your job, it's likely some effort will be made to transfer you into another position.*

*CASE STUDY: bye-bye manager*

One of us found ourselves in an 'impossible boss' situation in the mid-nineties. We were working long hours with little recognition, making suggestions that were not being taken up and generally feeling that we were getting more interference than support from our line manager.

This state of affairs persisted for several months until things came to a head in a pretty confrontational performance review. We fully expected to have to find a new job, if we weren't sacked beforehand. But in fact the employer recognised the problem and moved us into a different team where, surprise, surprise, we were a lot happier and our career prospered.

*And the rest*

Dealing with communications, rewards, recognition and poor manager relationships are perhaps the key things that will help you to be happier at work, but what about the other four items in our list? Few options for personal development, ideas being ignored, lack of opportunities for good performers and lack of benefits? Some of these points have already been partially covered in the sections above, but here are some further pointers on each:

■ **Getting more personal development:** make training an item on your review agenda or point out ways in which your employer will benefit from sending you on courses. If the development is something you want to do anyway, you might want to offer to shoulder some of the cost or take unpaid leave to do it.

> *"Make training an item on your review agenda or point out ways in which your employer will benefit from sending you on courses."*

■ **Getting your ideas noticed:** try to take responsibility for seeing the idea through so that it's harder for others to claim authorship. Mention your ideas widely around the organisation so you become known as an inspired thinker. But also be careful to recognise other people's good ideas; that way they will (hopefully) return the favour.

■ **Get more opportunities:** put yourself forward for new projects and initiatives. Take every chance you can to acquire skills that you can use at work. Work closely with other teams or departments which might be able to offer you some kind of career progression.

■ **Get more benefits**: as mentioned previously, your employer might see additional benefits as a welcome alternative to pay increases so bear this in mind at review time. When thinking about benefits, the smart thing to do is to focus on those that help you *and* your employer. So, for example, you might be able to get your company to pay for your home internet connection if you can show that you will use it to get work done from home at the weekends. Remember that your own boss will almost certainly be constrained by a budget, so try to find out what can and cannot be achieved without complicating things for them.

## IF ALL ELSE FAILS

So you've tried all this … and none of it has worked? In that case, it may well be time to turn to plan B: getting another job. But first, we want to give you a little pep talk. After all, you want to go into job-hunting mode in a positive frame of mind, not thinking of it as a desperate last resort. That's why in the rest of this chapter we're going to take a quick look at why your current job may not be all it's cracked up to be … and why you may not be risking much if you try to leave. This isn't sour grapes, but an honest (trust us) appraisal of the real benefits of any, and all, forms of employment in today's work environment.

## Risky assumptions

Remember how at the beginning of the chapter we talked about the value of the monthly pay cheque, pension, car, private medical insurance, gym membership and so on? About how difficult it would be to give all this up?

The problem with this attitude is that it may be based on a false assessment of the risks at stake. Our minds are notoriously bad at evaluating risks, something which has been explored in depth by a number of authors. In their book *Freakonomics*[17], for example, economist Steven D. Levitt and writer Stephen J. Dubner describe how parents in the United States 'logically' assume that having a gun in the house will be potentially more dangerous for their kids than having a swimming pool — even though the number of children that drown in swimming pools every year is far, far greater than the number that die from gunshot wounds. A similar thing is going on here with your perceptions of job security.

Moving to a new job is always going to seem risky. Your job is that tranquil, shimmering swimming pool. And moving is that mortally dangerous gun. But this perception is nonsense, of course. As we know, no job is entirely secure. You could find yourself out of work at any time, for any number of reasons.

A change in strategic direction diminishes or eliminates your role in the company. A market crash or recession forces your employer to downsize. Poor management sends the business into administration.

17. Dubner, Stephen J. and Levitt, Steven D. (2006) *Freakonomics: A Rogue Economist Explores the Hidden Side of Everything*, Penguin, ISBN 0141019018.

# These are not rare occurrences. They happen every day, and are happening right now, to hundreds of people just like you.

And even while your job is (or appears to be) secure, you may be running a risk. Although perhaps a better term for it would be 'opportunity cost': the danger that you're missing out on something by not acting. Let's take an example here from one of our own experiences.

### Stuck in a rut

Many years ago, one of us was working for a large West End-based communications agency, editing corporate magazines for a select group of loyal clients. The work environment was great. A lively, supportive team, clients who were fun to work and socialise with, and all the attractions of London's buzzing Soho district on the doorstep at the end of the day. But the work itself, after a while, became less than stimulating. There is only a given amount of complexity involved in getting a company magazine out on time. Once you've mastered it, and repeated the process on a regular schedule for a number of years, the challenge it offers understandably diminishes.

This problem was raised with the boss, who was very understanding but said that at the end of the day he could not offer a change of role because the relationships the author had built up with his clients were too valuable to the business. It was a classic 'why should I work for you?' moment: the employer getting all the benefit at the expense of the employee, rather than the other way around. This author did not hang around for long afterwards, but by that point had already wasted a number of years in a job that was basically going nowhere.

### Other opportunity costs

Being pigeon-holed or locked into a role that prevents you from gaining personal advancement with an employer is one type of opportunity cost, but there are many others, including some which are perhaps a lot more familiar.

One of the most common is simply being in a position where the promotion path is blocked, where for example your boss's chances of ever moving on are virtually nil. This is particularly prevalent in small companies where quite literally there *is* no career path as there are so few people in the organisation.

Another instance might be where you work for an employer that is unnecessarily tight when it comes to training and development.

If you're in a line of work that requires you to be on top of new technical developments or the like, then you might find your options become more limited just by staying with your current employer. In the service sector, a similar problem might arise if you work for a company that does not handle the kinds of work or kinds of clients you're keen on.

*"If you're in a line of work that requires you to be on top of new technical developments or the like, then you might find your options become more limited just by staying with your current employer."*

### The cost of leaving

So where you are and what you're doing right now might not be quite as cushy as you think. But, surely, leaving it for something else is always going to be a lot more risky, right? What about the bills, the mortgage, the family? Isn't there a danger my new job could actually be worse than what I've got now? What if I can't find a better job? And won't employers be put off if I start hopping from one job to another? Well, let's see. And let's start with the last point first.

The recruitment company Michael Page says: 'We live in an age when the one-company individual no longer exists. Your father, mother or grandparents may have worked for one company their entire lives, but it's becoming commonplace to be employed by three, four or more companies during one's lifetime.'

'Up to a decade ago, interviewers frowned upon a résumé that betrayed you as a "job hopper". However, this attitude has started to shift … industries such as technology, advertising and PR … have elevated job-hopping to a lifestyle and a necessity to keep up with industry changes. In fact, according to one recruiter, in some industries if you stayed in the same job for five years you'd have some explaining to do.'[18]

Indeed, we now live in an unashamed, opportunity-seeking world where candidates leave their CVs online in vast numbers, using the web as their shop window. This style of passive job hunting is starting to overtake the more conventional route to finding your next employer.

**The more the merrier**
Speaking specifically about professionals in the Human Resources (HR) industry, Lynne Hardman, the managing director of Hays Human Resources, says: 'If you have been with one employer for ten years or more and have only progressed from, say, HR officer to HR manager, then that doesn't look good. To feel stretched, most HR practitioners tend to move on every five years or so. By moving to a different organisation, perhaps in a new sector, you can fill knowledge gaps. This can be a real CV strengthener.'[19]

The Indian writer Madhavan Gopalachary points out that: 'If people change jobs, it shows guts, ability to face hardships and prove oneself. Each job change means starting all over again and proving oneself in a different and new environment.'[20]

> *"If people change jobs, it shows guts, ability to face hardships and prove oneself."*

**You don't go places without going places**
Unsurprisingly, then, when Vodafone carried out research into the working culture in the United Kingdom, it found that only 3% of organisations still think a person who has worked for only a few employers is a loyal worker.[21]

*Tip: Think of people whom you consider successful or look up to at work. How many jobs have they had? Does the number of jobs they've had make them*

18. Michael Page International, 'Job-hopping – a leap forward for your career prospects or a giant step back?', from the Michael Page website: www.michaelpage.com/content.html?pageId=14346.
19. Quoted in *Personnel Today*, 6 December, 2005: 'Trends: job-hopping', by Kirstie Redford.
20. From Evan Carmichael: 'Job Hopping', Madhavan T. Gopalachary, June 2007.
   See www.evancarmichael.com/Management/1055/Job-Hopping.html.
21. From Loyalty at Work, part of Vodafone UK's Working Nation research series, quoted in *Personnel Today*, 10 July, 2007: 'How to: job hop', by Scott Beagrie.

*seem any less successful? Remember to take into account your Jobsite Personal
Profile here. If you're a supporter, for example, you're more likely to look up to
people with job stability than, say, a balancer.*

So, if changing jobs doesn't reflect badly on your CV, what is holding you
back? Ah yes: that small requirement for a decent pay and benefits package.
Well, let's start with the obvious. Since the idea is that you would only be
leaving to find something better, then presumably you will factor in an
improved package (or greater flexibility, or greater stability, or whatever it is
that you want right now) into the deal. And employers seem to be pretty
accommodating on this point. In fact, it's your single most likely time to get
your largest-ever pay rise, as companies very rarely decide to drop a chosen
candidate because of pay.

### The way out is the way up

While you may have to fight tooth and nail to get a miserly pay increase out
of your existing employer, put yourself on the job market and you could be
wooed with a range of sumptuous welcoming incentives. According to the
Chartered Institute of Personnel and Development, more than 4 out of 10
employers will increase starting salaries and/or benefits packages when
they're experiencing recruitment difficulties (and over two thirds of those
say it works, too)[22].

More than a third[23] will provide flexible working packages and more than 1
in 10[24] will treat you to a golden hello, a strategy which works for more than
half[25] of organisations that offer it. (You may be glad to know that only 5%
will consider sending the job offshore if they cannot get the right candidate
straight away.)

### Know what you want

What this underscores, however, is that if you're going to get a better deal
by moving on then you have to have a clear idea of what you want and clear
reasons for wanting it. Writing in *Personnel Today*, journalist Scott Beagrie

---

22. From the 2008 annual survey report on recruitment, retention and turnover from the Chartered Institute of
    Personnel and Development.  Redford.
23. 36%, from the same report.
24. 14%, from the same report.
25. 52%, from the same report

says: 'Think about why you want to job hop—it's important to have the correct motivation. Is it to improve career prospects, earn more money, acquire specialist skills and knowledge, work in a nicer location or to find a better fit for your values?

'These are all valid reasons, but hopping aimlessly because you're bored or fed up will not do you or your CV any favours. Remember, future employers will want to know why you've moved jobs on a regular basis and you'll be in a stronger position if you can substantiate why. Organisations need to know that you're worthy of investment and not going to leave at the drop of a hat.'[26]

### Don't switch for the sake of it

In other words, switching jobs for the sake of it will not help your career. But using the ideas in this book, you can give your career progression a fundamental purpose that will attract, rather than scare, potential employers. Later in this book we will take a quick trip into the minds of these employers to find out exactly why they should be so willing to fall over themselves to get to you, and exactly how far they will be prepared to go in your pursuit. But first, a final thought for those of you still unsure about taking the plunge.

### Why it might be best to burn your bridges

In his book *Predictably Irrational* [27], the American behavioural economist Dan Ariely describes an intriguing experiment. Students were shown a screen with three doors and told that if they clicked on a given door they would get a payment within a certain range (say, one to five cents per click for one door and four to eight cents per click for another). They only had 100 clicks each, which they would obviously waste by clicking on doors that offered lower payouts. So most people clicked on all three doors a few times and then concentrated on the one that appeared to be giving the highest payout, as you might expect.

26. *Personnel Today*, 10 July 2007: 'How to: job hop', by Scott Beagrie.
27. Dan Ariely, *Predictably Irrational: The Hidden Forces That Shape Our Decisions*, HarperCollins, ISBN 9780007256525. Not really a book on how to get the job you want, but a jolly interesting read nevertheless.

Then the researchers changed the rules so that if you didn't click on a door for a while then it would disappear. They found that people just had to keep going back and clicking on each door before it disappeared, even if they knew the door would only give them a low payout and they were losing valuable clicks in the process. Further, if it actually cost money to click on door (even one that would yield a low-value payout), people would still make sure it remained available. In the end the experimenters actually told the subjects which door would yield most money and which one least. But the subjects still insisted on wasting clicks on doors which were not worth the effort[28].

## When one door closes
What the researchers concluded is that we have an irrational fear of closing doors, burning our bridges. In some cases, of course, it might pay to keep our options open. But if we really, deep down, know that a particular path is leading us nowhere, perhaps it's time to 'fess up to the fact that we are acting irrationally, and it's time to close the door.

29. In actual fact the experimenters went to even further lengths to show how pointless it was to click on low-value doors, but the end result was the same in all cases.

CHAPTER 5:
# Snaring your ideal job

**What you'll get out of this chapter:**
- ◼ *Ten things you should know about yourself in order to pursue your ideal career.*
- ◼ *Half a dozen great ways to fill your ideas bank with job possibilities.*
- ◼ *Six questions to ask about the role you're hoping to win.*

WHAT did you want to be when you were a kid? Pop star? Nurse? Astronaut? Were you determined to follow that path, come what may? Looking back on it now, it's probably obvious why you could never have been what you wanted at age seven or eight. As we get older, we all make choices which ultimately narrow down our career possibilities. A maths degree sets us on the path to accountancy. A summer job ends up getting us into office administration. A typing course turns us into a secretary. Before you know it, our chances of becoming that pop star, nurse or astronaut are basically nil. Or are they?

What we're going to do now might not be quite as dramatic as playing Wembley Stadium or orbiting Earth, but it could be pretty impressive nevertheless. We are going to conjure up a new job for ourselves. One that we feel comfortable with and we will be good at. One that will give us the rewards we want. One that will make us happy. And once we have worked out what it is, we will go and get it. Are you ready?

## WHAT WORK WILL WORK FOR YOU?

Let's start by going back to the exercises that we looked at earlier in the book. Before you start rushing to check what jobs are available, you're going to need to have a clear idea of what you really want to do. After all, the employers you're going to be targeting are not just posting job descriptions for the sake of it. They will have worked out a detailed list of requirements that

*"Before you start rushing to check what jobs are available, you're going to need to have a clear idea of what you really want to do."*

candidates will need to meet. If you're going to get what *you* want, you need to be just as thorough about the things you will expect from your prospective employer. So grab a sheet of paper and start to list what you know about yourself and your job (and life) aspirations. It might look a bit like this:

1. What is my current job, role and area of responsibility?

2. How happy am I at work right now, and what areas am I most unhappy with? (Refer to the Happy Days test in Chapter 1 for this.)

3. What is my Jobsite Personal Profile and what does that mean I want out of my career? (Refer to Chapter 3.)

4. What are my main strengths? (See Chapter 2.)

5. What are my biggest achievements/the things I have been proudest of? (See Chapter 2.)

6. What motivates me? (See Chapter 2 again.)

7. What has attracted me to jobs up until now? (Also take a look at your ideas bank here[30]; are there any things in common with the jobs or careers you're interested in?)

8. What has been missing from my current job and/or other jobs before? (Now write the opposite of all these things and you will have a description of the kinds of things you might want in a job.)

9. What is my personality type and what attributes does it give me that are relevant to my career? (See Chapter 2.)

10. What are my core values? (See Chapter 2 again.)

Once you have answered all the questions, you might end up with something like this:

---

30. This was introduced back in chapter 2.

1. What is my current job, role and area of responsibility?
   - *Communications manager in a large multinational.*

2. How happy am I at work right now, and what areas am I most unhappy with? (Refer to the test in Chapter 1 for this.)
   - From the Happy Days test: *'You may pretend to yourself that work is so-so, but the truth is that you're far less happy than you will admit.*

   *Although you tell yourself that things aren't too bad, they're dragging you down. It could be that you're not as well-paid as you think you deserve to be, but that you feel it's a sign of greed to complain about cash.*

   *Work shouldn't, and doesn't, have to be this way. Don't suffer in silence and don't stubbornly decide to tough it out. Research has shown that being unhappy at work can have a real impact on your physical health.*

   *Whatever happens, don't fail to address problems like this - you owe it to yourself to be happy at work.*

   *If you find ways to make your work life better, your whole life will work better.'*

3. What is my Jobsite Personal Profile and what does that mean I want out of my career? (Refer to Chapter 3.)

   - From Jobsite Personal Profile: *Contender*

*As a Contender, you're likely to believe at times it's necessary for work to come before the family, with the knowledge that the family will benefit in the long run from your success.*

*You believe that in a world of opportunities, the strongest thrive. Fortunately, you're a person that makes things happen. You're able to set goals and focus on achieving them, not afraid to make difficult decisions or take risks. The last thing you want is a dead end job, you want to move on up and be rewarded for your efforts and ability.*

4. What are my main strengths?
   - *Creativity, enthusiasm and quick thinking.*

5. What are my biggest achievements/the things I have been proudest of?
   – *Successful launch of a newsletter, structural changes in the way the organisation works, providing ideas that have been taken up by others.*

6. What motivates me?
   – *Promotion, more money, recognition.*

7. What has attracted me to jobs up until now? (Also take a look at your ideas bank here; are there any things in common with the jobs or careers you're interested in?)
   – *Opportunities to learn, prestige, money.*

8. What has been missing from your current job and/or other jobs before? (Now write the opposite of all these things and you will have a description of the kinds of things you might want in a job.)
   – *Independence, room to develop my career, a decent salary.*

9. What is your personality type and what attributes does it give you that are relevant to your career? (See Chapter 2)
   – *ESFP: enjoy new experiences, good people skills, like having fun, independent, spontaneous, dislike routines and theory, easily bored.*

10. What are your core values?
    – *Creativity, freedom, excitement, fairness.*

What emerges from the above list is a portrait of someone who is unhappy at work and craves greater independence and creativity in a more rewarding environment, with the opportunity to use their people skills and spontaneity to face new challenges.

Your list will be different, of course, but it should give you a similar idea of what is missing from your work life and what you need to look for in your next job.

## YOUR ULTIMATE OBJECTIVE

This list gives you two things: a starting point (who and where you are now) and a direction of travel (what sorts of things you would need to have in order to be satisfied with your future career). Now let's try to find your ultimate destination[31]. For this, imagine a point in the future (it doesn't really matter when) at which you have achieved all you ever wanted. Think of the kind of house you will live in. Think of where it will be. Think of the people you will live with, and the people you will know. Think of what you will do with your time. How you will feel when you get up in the morning or go about your daily business.

Throughout all this, do not worry about being too specific with the details. Rather than say 'I'd like to live in a detached house on the outskirts of Salford', it's more a question of 'I'd like a large comfortable home in a quiet neighbourhood in a place that has special meaning for me.'

## FUTURE PERFECT

Once you've got an idea of what your perfect future life might look like, turn to your future perfect job. Again, leave out specifics, but try to think in general terms about things such as:

■ What kind of environment you will work in? Do you see yourself in a pin-striped suit striding through a busy City office? Working at your own pace at home? Enduring the elements outdoors?

■ What kind of organisation will you work in? Will it be a big, fast-paced corporation? A hungry, ambitious start-up? A public sector or voluntary body?

■ Which of your strengths will you use at work? Will you rely on your ability to talk to people? To be creative? To organise things?

■ Who will you work with? Executives? Students? The general public?

31. Much of what comes next draws loosely on the Firework programme developed by Marianne Craig. (See Chapter 2)

**Picture yourself**

Other things you could ask yourself are what kind of location you see yourself in; whether you will be travelling much or at all; who you will work for; what sort of schedule you will follow; what kinds of things you will do in your working day; and so on. Also, think about how this as-yet-undetermined job will make you feel: Secure? Respected? Challenged?

*"Think about how this as-yet-undetermined job will make you feel: Secure? Respected? Challenged?"*

Now you've got an image of the perfect career, in the same way as an employer builds up an image of the perfect candidate for a job. The next phase is to start looking for roles that might be able to provide you with this perfect career.

*Tip: Don't start looking at specific employers just yet. That comes almost at the end of the process, in the same way as an employer draws up a shortlist of candidates only after casting a net far and wide to search for applicants.*

**Raid your ideas bank**

The best place to start your search is with your ideas bank. Remember that this was a list (or perhaps an envelope, file or folder) where you kept track of any and all interesting job or career openings that caught your eye. These could be as specific as a job advert on a recruitment website to as vague as a newspaper feature on a place you felt you would like to work in.

If you've been trying to fill your ideas bank diligently then you should have at least two or three dozen items in it. If you don't, then you might want to spend some time thinking up some more examples to include. You can do this by:

■ Searching on recruitment websites.

■ Scanning employment sections of newspapers and magazines.

■ Seeing what careers would be a natural fit for your personality type (see Chapter 2).

■ Thinking about characters you identify with in books, films or TV series, and noting their occupations.

■ Listing the occupations of friends and family members who do things that you envy or respect.

■ Thinking about careers connected to the things you admire or enjoy in life.

Now let's take a look at what you have accumulated so far. Here's a sample list that we have dreamt up for the purposes of illustration, based on the preferences of one of us:

■ Marine biologist
■ Lecturer
■ Architect
■ Creative web designer, £30,000, Central London
■ Creative web designer, £35k pa, Hampshire
■ Producer, £28-32K + bonus + package, London, Top 10 Digital Creative Marketing Agency
■ Strategist, £35k-£50k pa + excellent package, Brighton
■ Our busy bid team requires an additional proposal writer to join our expanding international company in Mitcheldean, Gloucestershire
■ Anthropologist
■ Desktop publishing specialist
■ Crime Scene Investigation
■ Photographer
■ Blog author
■ Consultant in a think tank or consultancy body
■ Archaeologist
■ Travel writer
■ Animator
■ Producer sought by small London production company
■ Magazine layout sub-editor
■ Sherlock Holmes!!
■ Games software developer: £Excellent, immediate incorporation
■ Writing comedy sketches for the BBC?
■ Course number 6.034: Artificial Intelligence
■ Artificial life creator

- Reviewer
- Inventor?
- Record cover designer??
- Illustrator
- Cartoonist
- Set up a small business

*"At first sight, your list might seem a bit bewildering."*

### Full theme ahead

We expect that your list will probably be very different to this one. But note the following: anything goes. The list includes actual job ads, rough ideas and thoughts, and even things that are only vaguely connected with work (such as a TV series, a fictional character and an open university course). At first sight, your list might seem a bit bewildering. But remember, these aren't jobs you're actually going to apply for. They are clues to the kinds of things you're attracted to.

So your task now is to go through them and look for underlying links and themes. What things do the contents of your ideas bank have in common?

If you look through the list above, which includes ideas as unrelated as web designer and crime scene investigator, you might notice certain basic trends. For example:
- Many of the types of work listed involve a lot of autonomy, not much teamwork.
- They tend to be about dealing with things rather than people.
- Some of them involve a degree of creativity and problem-solving.

And so on. Clearly, the person who put together this ideas bank is not going to be very happy working with people all the time in a fairly inflexible environment.

### *Looking for clues*

Your ideas bank should throw up important pointers to what attracts you to certain types of work. If you have lots of ideas in your bank, you may be able to pull out lots and lots of underlying themes. Some of them may even appear to be contradictory. Don't worry.

# When you've got as many themes as you can, take a step back and try to work out which three or four are most important to you.

### What your employer needs to give you

What have you got? Maybe your themes are 'working with children' or 'using my analytical skills' or 'creating something that will have a lasting impact'. Now think of what kinds of jobs will best fit these themes. You are close to having an idea of what your perfect employer will have to offer you in order to answer the question 'Why should I work for you?' If they cannot provide the things that really matter to you, then frankly you will not be happy working for them. (And, let's face it, that's the attitude that employers have long had with job candidates.)

Having worked out what you want your future employer to look like, now is the time to go out and find them. In some respects, however, the next step is the most difficult. After you have thought long and hard about why you should move and where you should move to, it's sometimes easy to sink back into inaction. The mortgage still needs paying, so you won't change jobs just yet. There is a change in management, so you will hang on a bit longer to see how things pan out. The job market is looking a bit shaky right now, so best not do anything rash.

> *"Having worked out what you want your future employer to look like, now is the time to go out and find them."*

## GET OFF YOUR BUTT

Wake up! What have we been telling you so far? You've worked out exactly how and why you're unhappy in your job. You know that moving jobs is not such a big deal after all. And you know exactly what it is you want to do now. This is not a trivial part of your life that we're talking about here. It is nine-to-five (or thereabouts) of nearly two thirds of every year in your working life. The only other activity you will dedicate so much time to (if you're lucky) is sleeping.

*Tip: Don't waste a second longer. Start looking for jobs* now *that can offer you what you want. It's going to take time and effort to get your career straightened out, but the payback will be immense. Chances are you will be a lot happier, meet more like-minded people and become more successful in a matter of months.*

## FROM THOUGHT TO ACTION

What kinds of work fit in with the themes you've uncovered? Whatever they are, it's possible that they might not be things you can transfer into straight away. If you're a nurse right now and you think you might want to become an airline pilot then the chances are you're going to find it a bit of an uphill struggle. You basically have two options.

The first is to look again at your chosen theme and see if there is something else that matches it and which is perhaps a better fit to your skills and experience. For instance, if you want to be an airline pilot purely because you enjoy travelling abroad and do not want a fixed nine-to-five, then maybe you could look at becoming a cabin crew member instead (in which case your nursing experience would probably be seen as a positive asset).

The second option is to build a plan of action to get you to the job you want. This might involve, for example:
- Taking voluntary redundancy.
- Investing my redundancy money in flight training.
- Getting a job in airline or airport operations if I cannot find a pilot's job immediately.

Note that even the act of moving to a job that is a small step towards what you really want to do will still help you to be happier and more successful at work, since it will fulfil more of the criteria that matter to you.

*"Even the act of moving to a job that is a small step towards what you really want to do will still help you to be happier."*

## CLOSING DOORS

An important part of the exercises we have gone through so far is that they will also help you to identify what *not* to do. Keep a note of what you have ruled out. This is your no-go zone. It will help you organise your thoughts and give you reassurance that you're making real progress towards the kind of work that will work for you. You may have just heard of an opening that will pay you a lot better, for example.

But if what you really value is more flexibility and a better work-life balance, and the higher-paid job does not offer that, then the chances are you will be disappointed and unhappy at work no matter how much you're earning.

## TIME TO GET TO WORK

So you know (roughly) what you want to do. What do you do next to find the right job? When an employer has a vacancy, they study the market, put together a package which they think will be attractive, then attract and interview candidates for the post. You're going to do exactly the same. What do you know about the roles that fit in with your core work themes? (Bear in mind that at this stage there may be a variety of jobs that would work for a particular theme.) If they're unfamiliar to you, then read up all you can about them. Scan the internet, buy industry publications, talk to people who work in them.

When looking at potential roles to apply to, try to answer questions such as:
- How much money do these roles pay?
- What are the working conditions?
- What kinds of qualifications or skills do they require?
- What is the usual entry route into these jobs?
- What kinds of personality profile do they fit best?
- Who are the main employers?

## KNOW YOUR EMPLOYER

This process of investigation may help you to narrow down your list of potential roles and employers. For example, if you're keen on teaching then you might find that working for a training company is more likely to fit your personality and circumstances than, say, working in the education sector.

It will also help you to understand what you'll need to provide in order to appeal to your chosen employer. As we will see later on, being seen to fit in is an important part of getting an employer on your side, and nothing can help you fit in as much as having an in-depth knowledge of the employer's market and operations.

## A MATCH MADE ON PAPER

We will come onto the dos and don'ts of CV writing and making a good impression later on. But for now, once you have carried out a reasonable amount of research into your chosen target career route in, say, advertising, you might want to draw up a list something like this:

| | What employer can offer | What I have/want |
|---|---|---|
| Salary | Usually c. £30k | Need £35k min |
| Hours | 9 to 5 | Flexible work |
| Location | Jobs in local area | Cannot relocate |
| Prospects | Promotion after 1-2 years | Would want rapid progress |
| Training | On the job | I already have qualifications |
| Perks | Negotiable | I need pension |

*Tip: Try to include as many things as you can think of, as this will help you further narrow down your shortlist of jobs and employers, and may ultimately form the basis of your detailed contract negotiations when you find a suitable employer.*

## THE SEARCH IS ON

Your research should also reveal which employers operate in your chosen field, and how they usually recruit. Of course, now is the time to start looking out for relevant job ads. Check industry publications, sign up to recruitment websites and set up alerts for your chosen employers and job descriptions. Bear in mind a particular job may go under a variety of guises.

# Tell your computer! Recruitment websites will allow you to perform keyword searches that will capture the roles you're looking for.

Don't just limit yourself to looking for existing openings, however. Bear in mind that whenever a job is advertised, a large number of candidates may apply, especially if it's in a competitive sector. Recruitment agencies and human resources departments spend a lot of time throwing out applications from candidates who are clearly not very well suited to the role advertised. You do not want to be one of these, of course (and more of this further on), but even so you have to be aware that you will face a lot of competition if you only approach employers when they're publicly advertising a job.

## OTHER STRATEGIES

What else can you do, then? Well, if employers advertise when they need employees, why don't you advertise when you need an employer? We are not talking about putting a display ad in the local paper, of course. But there is no harm in going direct to the people who might be able to offer you a job, and letting them know you're available and interested.

*"There is no harm in going direct to the people who might be able to offer you a job."*

Ways in which you can approach employers directly include:
- Contact relevant organisations and find out what their recruitment intentions are. See if you can get your foot in the door by having them put your CV on file, or even request a speculative interview.
- If your dream job role is one that is often filled by agencies or head-hunters, make sure you're on their books and talk to them frequently to find out what's available.
- If appropriate to the role and the employer (and assuming you have the ability), offer to do some work experience or participate in a project on a pro-bono basis.
- Leave your CV online for employers to find you. That way you will be job seeking around the clock and doubling the impact of your own efforts. You'll also reach employers who may not have advertised the vacancy.

When you're contacting employers, do not be afraid to pick up the phone. Clearly, HR professionals are busy people and may not always have the time to talk to you. But if you're courteous and it's clear that you're interested in understanding their business, with a view to making a valuable contribution, then you may be able to build up a rapport and get worthwhile information and feedback at the same time.

Also find out whether there are relevant industry or business groups you can join that will help you come into contact with these employers.

## A FOOT IN THE DOOR

A young professional known to one of us had an unusual but effective way of getting work. He would brazenly contact people he admired in the world of business and request an interview with them 'to help me with my career'. The people concerned (some of whom were fairly significant captains of industry) were usually flattered by the request and often spared him half an hour or so of their time. Not only did he gain valuable insights into the workings of big business (and how he could further his career in it) but he also ended up with an impressive list of personal contacts that he was able to use when talking about work opportunities.

## PLAN A MARKETING CAMPAIGN

All the above should be fine if you've got time on your hands to find your perfect job. But if you're trying to break into a hard-to-find role, or need to find employment soon, or simply want to maximise your chances of getting an interview, then you might want to take a more structured approach to finding your employer. One way to do this is to emulate what employers do in recruitment campaigns, and create your own 'recruiter campaign'. Here is how you can do it:

- Draw up a prospect list of potential employers. Keep it fairly wide to begin with, including employers that might be able to offer roles similar to the one you're looking for.

- Do research to find out who to contact at each one regarding jobs, and how they prefer to be communicated with.

- Assemble your 'sales collateral': personalised covering letters, tailored CVs and any supporting material you might need, such as copies of certificates or case studies of projects you have been involved in. (We'll come onto this in due course.)

- Contact the people on your prospect list in the most appropriate way. Be sure to mention that you intend to follow up with them shortly to gauge their level of interest.

- Follow up within a few days. The best way to do this is by phone if you can, since (provided you're always courteous) it allows you to establish a personal rapport with the employer.

- Always try to close your pitch with a gentle push for an interview, even if it's under the guise of 'taking 10 minutes of your time to get to know your business better'. Be prepared to be flexible with timings: 'If things are busy now, how about I call back in a couple of weeks?' 'I live nearby so I could drop by briefly at breakfast time if you're in early...'

■ It may take several attempts or more to get your foot in any particular door. Be polite and persistent. Also, it might be difficult to call potential employers when you're at your current place of work, so you will need to be careful in your timing.

■ Use the same techniques when you're responding to a job ad online or in the press.

■ Put together a timetable and stick to it. Just like you would do at work. The deadlines you get given by your boss may be annoying but they're also a massively helpful way of making sure things get done. So pretend your manager has given you this as an assignment. It may be just what you need to see the process through.

## TIME TO DUST OFF THE INTERVIEW SUIT

Every employer knows they have to offer a decent package in order to attract the right candidates. In the world where you control the employment process, it's important that you offer a decent package to attract the right employer. Exactly how you do that is the subject of the next chapter.

CHAPTER 6:

# Why you should hire me – part one

**What you'll get out of this chapter:**
- ■ *Six steps for turning your so-so CV into a real employer attention-grabber.*
- ■ *Seven CV sins that you should stay away from at all costs.*
- ■ *Four rules you need to apply to all the items in your job application.*

EMPLOYERS that want to boast the best employees go to some lengths to put together an attractive package for new recruits. Now you're controlling the employment process, it's up to you to put together an attractive package to lure your ideal employer. Thankfully, you have already done most of the hard work. The exercises in earlier chapters will have helped you work out what your main skills and strengths are.

The research you will have carried out as detailed previously will give you a good idea of what prospective employers look for in the area you're interested in breaking into. All you need to do now is match your skills to an employer's requirements.

## MATCHING SKILLS TO JOBS

There might not be an obvious match to begin with. You may need to think hard about how your skills and experience can be shown to match an employer's needs. For example, a job description may ask for team-working skills while you currently work on your own. Fair enough, but can you come up with any other evidence of teamwork? Have you successfully assembled a group of suppliers or partners for a specific project? Captained a sports team? Traditionally taken the lead in team-building away days? Bear in mind that if the job you're after really matches

*"You may need to think hard about how your skills and experience can be shown to match an employer's needs."*

your interests and aspirations then it's highly likely that you will have done something related to it in the past, perhaps as part of a hobby or course of study. To organise your selling points, you might want to draw up a table like this:

| Employer's requirements | My skills/experience |
| --- | --- |
| Demonstrate you're self-motivated | Current job involves me starting my own projects |
| Be a good communicator | Led debating team at college |
| Build rapport with customers and colleagues | I have to pull together teams in my projects now |
| Articulate information and ideas clearly | I write project briefs as part of my job |
| Respond to questions accurately | Score in college exams was highest in class |
| Communicate the benefits of our product range | I have to sell benefits of my current projects |
| Demonstrate good active listening | Point to part-time work fundraising for the Samaritans |
| Do the right thing for our customers | Used to work on customer complaints help line |
| Treat others fairly and consistently | See my experience in project teams |
| Handle customer issues in a positive manner | See experience in customer complaints |

Note that you will probably want to have more than one strength or skill for each requirement; try to make your list as complete as possible. You will use this to create killer CVs and covering letters and it will give you all the ammunition you need to grab an employer's attention during your interview(s).

Note also that you should write a separate list for each employer, since different jobs will have differing requirements and individual employers will place different levels of emphasis on different skills.

## ARE YOU A PERSON OR A FISH?

When fish breed, they usually lay thousands (sometimes millions) of eggs and then head off to do fishy things, leaving their offspring to fend for themselves. Unsurprisingly, most of the eggs end up becoming fish food and only a few of them reach adulthood. People, in contrast, only have a few children but invest massive amounts of time, effort and money to ensure they reach adulthood unscathed.

Both approaches can be applied to looking for a job. You can use a scattergun approach and go for as many jobs as possible in the hope that an employer will eventually make you an offer. Or you can focus your efforts on just a few employers in order to maximise your chances of one of them taking you on.

*"Focus your efforts on just a few employers in order to maximise your chances of one of them taking you on."*

## IMPROVE YOUR CHANCES OF GETTING THE JOB YOU WANT

The reason we would advocate taking the second route is that if you're fairly certain of the job you want to get, and have a good knowledge of potential employers, then it's unlikely you will have a massive range of targets to choose from. The fish approach works best for people who really do not have much of a clue about what they want to do and do not mind trying to get a job with all and sundry. If you have read this far, then we suspect your thinking is probably a little more highly evolved.

## SELLING YOURSELF

In order to maximise your chances of success with a particular employer, you're going to need to hit them with a killer CV or job application. We'll come onto the job application bit in a minute; let's focus on the CV for now, since this is probably the most critical document you will need in order to approach an employer.

So what is a CV? Is it a record of your experience and achievements? A showcase for your skills and knowledge? A summary of your work and education to date? Well, it's all of those things. But primarily it's something completely different: a way of selling yourself to a potential employer. It is crucial that you understand this, because winning CVs are the ones that do the best job of selling the candidate, not the ones that provide the best summary of work or record of experience. (Incidentally, this applies equally to covering letters, application forms and your behaviour in interviews. More on this later.)

Because your CV is all about selling, in many ways it has more in common with a good advert than it does with a list or summary. To write your killer CV, you need to look at the task through the eyes of an adman.

# You are the product. Your future employer is the customer. How do you get them to buy?

## MARKETING YOURSELF

The ad industry has invested millions of pounds in this very question for many decades, so it pays to take a leaf out of its book. Ad men (and women) almost never embark on an ad campaign until they have developed a thorough understanding of a product's customers and their needs. Simplifying greatly, the process they follow is more or less like this:
- Find out what problems matter to the customer.
- Find out how the product can solve these problems.
- Tell the customer about the solution in as persuasive a way as possible.

In your case, the first stage of this process has already been carried out by your potential employer. They know what they need and (if you're answering an employment ad) will have written it down in the job description.

*Tip: If you're making a speculative approach to an employer, your exact role within the business might not be so obvious. But with the research you have done so far you should at least have an idea of the kind of skills that would make you a valuable addition to their workforce.*

## CREATE A KILLER CV

What goes into your CV? Look back at the list you made earlier. Of all the things you think your prospective employer wants, try to work out which are the most important to them. Try to put yourself in the job that you're applying for and imagine what you would have to do on a day-to-day basis. Hopefully, your research into the role will help you a lot with this. If you're stumped, you might want to call the employer to get some more details. Pick the top two or three requirements for the job and see what skills and experience you have that are relevant to them.

These are the things that need to go right up front in your CV. One way of doing this is to start with a section called 'Key skills and experience' (or something similar). Provide a one-paragraph snapshot of yourself that mentions your main selling points. Then, throughout the rest of the CV, try to include all your other skills and experience relevant to the job.

### Arranging your CV

How should you order the information on your CV? Bearing in mind that this is basically an ad aimed at selling you to your employer, lead with the information that is most relevant to them, then include any other information that might also be relevant to them, and finally ditch anything irrelevant. There is plenty of advice available on how to put together a CV. You can even find online tools such as www.cvproducer.com that will help you put together a professional-looking CV. But the basic rule is always: keep it relevant to the job, and, just like that ad, keep it short. Without squeezing the text down so much that the reader will need a magnifying glass, you know you're onto a great CV structure if you can fit it on one or two sides of A4 paper.

# Let your skills and achievements speak for themselves.

Filling a CV with lots of detail may initially seem like a good way of selling yourself, but in fact the opposite is true. If you include everything down to the grades you got in your GCSEs, the person who reads your CV will either wonder why you haven't got anything more interesting to say for yourself, or fall asleep (or both). Now let's look at the information that you *do* need to include.

*"Filling a CV with lots of detail may initially seem like a good way of selling yourself, but in fact the opposite is true."*

### Contact details

Of course your name and contact details are of primary importance, so make sure they're immediately obvious on your CV. One way to do this is to include them in the header of your document. Make sure your name stands out but resist the temptation to put it (or any other information, for that matter) in gigantic bold letters right across the entire page. A more restrained or understated approach will usually convey more of an impression of professionalism and confidence. In your contact details, do not forget to include your full address and postcode, your email address and landline and/or mobile phone numbers (choose whichever you're most comfortable being contacted on but make sure there is a way for people to leave messages). If you're worried about the security of giving people access to your personal details, remember that the Data Protection Act will ensure the information on your CV will only be used for the purpose it is intended.

# Be wary of including your current work email address if your existing employer is not aware you're looking for jobs.

*Tip: Avoid confidential information such as your passport or national insurance numbers as these would never be required or requested at this stage of the job application process. Your age is also no longer required as the law protects against age discrimination during the recruitment process.*

### Key skills and experience

As mentioned above, including a special section with a title such as this gives you the opportunity to hit your employer between the eyes with all the reasons why they should hire you. Make this section short (one paragraph should do it) and factual. Concentrate on your achievements, not your responsibilities. If you're asking 'Why should I work for you?' then think of this section as saying 'This is why you should hire me'.

### Career summary

Unless you're a student, the next most important thing you will need to show in order to snare your employer is a list of your work achievements. Work back from the present in chronological order and for each job try to think of, and accentuate, anything you did that might be relevant to the role you're applying for now. Add in or leave out part-time or short-term jobs depending on whether you think they will help you sell yourself to this particular employer.

### Education and qualifications

Are you smart or what? If you're really, really smart then you probably don't need to make a big deal about it. Limit yourself to mentioning the Harvard MBA and the PhDs from Oxford and Cambridge. If you're pretty smart then make yourself look really, really smart by not making a big deal about it. Just mention your bachelor's degree from De Montfort, with a smattering of detail about your grades and courses.

> *"If you're really, really smart then you probably don't need to make a big deal about it."*

*Tip: Didn't go to college? No problem. Make yourself look pretty smart by briefly describing how many exams you passed at school and then including a line such as 'Passed over higher education to go direct to full-time employment'.*

Note the common theme here. Employers are, in general, not really interested in how many GCSEs or what 'A' grades you got at school. They just want to know whether you're smart (or at least smart enough to do the job). And a lot of that impression comes through in your confidence in limiting yourself to your finest achievements. The exception to this rule is where you have academic or vocational qualifications that are directly relevant to the role you're applying to.

These are obviously a lot more important than any others, so make sure they're at the top of your list. If you're applying for a job as a computer systems analyst, your 'A' level computer science is probably just as relevant as your degree in English literature, if not more so. (To be on the safe side, you might also add that you took an optional computer course at college, if that was the case.)

### Other information
Include here all the itsy-bitsy stuff your employer should know. Do you speak any languages? Hold any honorary posts? Have a driving licence?

# Try to think of what will raise you above the competition.

Also, this is the section where you might want to include information about hobbies and interests. Be careful with this one! Listing two or three fascinating pastimes ('wreck diving', 'breaking world records') might give you some great talking points in an interview. But at the same time beware that some of your heartiest passions ('playing golf' or 'going to the cinema') might not make you look that interesting on paper. And others ('train spotting', 'cider drinking') might actually harm your chances of getting a job. One of us recently saw a candidate whose CV listed 'arctic explorer' as a hobby. The entry worked very well for him indeed.

Be especially careful about listing anything which might invoke strong loyalty, such as dedication to a particular religion, political party or sports club.

### References
Not all applications will require them but it's always helpful to say that you can provide references on request.

# Make sure you have two or three people in the frame to provide these references before you offer them to prospective employers.

## Smarten up your CV

Once you have got all the information together, what should your CV look like? Our advice is to aim for a professional look by using clear headings and easily legible type. Resist the temptation to use fancy fonts. Apart from anything, if you're sending people your CV in Microsoft Word format, their computer may not support the typeface you have used and your document could end up looking distinctly odd.

Above all, try to keep your CV to just one side of A4 paper in length. Two sides is acceptable, one is best. 'But, but …!' we hear you splutter. No. Not a word more. Anything you cannot fit onto two sides of A4 really isn't worth mentioning. 'What about my secondary school egg-and-spoon race award?' No. When was the last time you saw an ad that rambled on over the page? 'My priceless 8-track[32] collection?' Absolutely not. Listen: even Bill Gates can fit his entire career summary onto a single page[33]. So why can't you?

*"By all means help your CV stand out from the pile, but don't do anything that will be annoying."*

## Death by design

Next, what about flashy borders, use of colour and other design touches? Well, the rule here is: by all means help your CV stand out from the pile, but don't do anything that will be annoying and/or run counter to the impression you're trying to convey. Online job boards may also not be able to send your CV if it's in a jazzed-up format. At the end of the day, most employers want to recruit a safe pair of hands, which means a capable, professional person. So you do not want your CV to make you look like a joker.

Should you include a photo? Nahhhh. Unless, that is, if you're applying for a job as a TV presenter, model or something else where your looks are really important. In which case, don't put the photo on the CV. Instead, include a professionally-taken large-scale print with your application.

---

32. Never heard of it? Look up 'Stereo 8' on Wikipedia.
33. Yes he really can. See http://www.microsoft.com/presspass/exec/billg/?tab=biography. And he even admits to enjoying golf. So maybe that's not so bad after all.

*Tip: If you're sending your CV out in the post then invest in some quality stationery.*

## A CV makeover

Let's see how a bit of thought can improve a CV. On the next page is a fairly standard CV. Following it is the same document with a few additional touches[34]. See if you can see what we have done … and which you think works better?

---

34. In case you're interested, yes this is a real CV, although of course we have permission from the owner and have changed the name, personal and employer details.

Annie Body
Home Address
1360 Holbrook Road
Stratford
London E15 3AB
Email: anniebody@whyshouldiworkforyou.com
Tel: 020 7946 0000
Date of Birth: 03.08.1972                          Nationality: British

**Employment**
**Megabank Finance: January 2000 to July 2007**
I have performed several roles at the company as follows:

**September 2004 to July 2007 – Authorisations Department non routine Case Officer.**
In this role I assessed non–routine applications for authorisation against the threshold conditions
and made recommendations for either approval or refusal. The assessment would involve
corresponding with firms to clarify aspects of the application but could also include visiting the
firm, interviewing senior management and working with third parties to ascertain the veracity of the
information provided. Internally I worked closely with the Supervision, Intelligence and
Enforcement areas and would also present cases for refusal to the Regulatory Transactions
Committee and the Regulatory Decision Committee.

My area of expertise was within the retail sector including electronic money issuers though I also
have experience of the wholesale sector. The role required extensive knowledge of the company
handbooks and rules and how these applied to each individual firm. The key skills for the roll were;
Strong analytical skills, precise written and oral communication including being able to present and
argue your case in front of committees and senior management, good case and time management,
good understanding of the regulations and their application, the ability to manage stakeholders both
internally and externally (including good customer service).

**June 2006 to July 2007 – Departmental Financial Crime Representative.**
As well as the above responsibilities, during this period, I dedicated 20% of my time to financial
crime issues. This role included meeting with other departments to assess financial crime risks and
being a focal point within the department for financial crime issues including queries and staff
training.

**April 2004 to September 2004 – Pensions Review Specialist.**
This was a varied role in which I took on many different responsibilities. The aim was to ensure
that the Pension Review was adequately completed. There were three main strands of work I was
involved with:

■ Supervision of the remaining firms that had not completed their Pension Review's and were
   able to do so.

■ Providing guidance and support to the loss assessment outsourcers on calculation
   methodology, interpretation of procedures and Pensions Review guidance in general.

■ Completion of the remaining loss assessments which remained in house.

**October 2003 to April 2004 – Pensions Review Team Coordinator.**
Managing a team of 12 people including dealing with performance issues and producing regular
management information and statistics.

I also responded to investor correspondence and queries, signed off loss assessments, updated procedures and attended technical meetings to discuss any issues that had been identified from day to day work or other sources.

**November 2001 to October 2003 – Pensions Review Calculations Sign Off.**

Signing off loss assessment calculations before writing to investors to inform them of the outcome. In this role I was also responsible for coaching less experienced team members and helping them with queries.

**January 2000 to November 2001 – Pensions Review Calculation Officer.**

Calculation of pensions review loss assessments as per the required guidelines and obtaining the required information from product providers, investors and pension schemes.

**Bigbank Life: May 1998 to January 2000**

Working within their new business department assessing new pension applications and liaising with Independent Financial Advisers (IFA's) to resolve any problems with these.

**Other**

Several other periods of temporary employment including 9 months within the Banking Insurance Institute.

**Qualifications**

2001 – Financial Planning Certificate (FPC) from the CII. This is the standard accreditation required to be a financial adviser.

September 1996 to September 1997 – MSc Environmental Science from Wye College (University of London).

September 1992 to July 1995 – BSc (2.2 Hons) Environmental Biology from Greenwich University.

September 1976 to July 1991 - 'A' Level passes in Biology, Chemistry and Spanish. O'Level Passes (C and above) in English, Spanish, Maths, Physics, Chemistry, Biology and Human Biology.

**Interests**

House renovation, the environment, gardening and music.

**Additional**

I am a fluent Spanish speaker and hold a clean driving licence. I am also competent in IT packages including Word, Excel and PowerPoint.

## CV Annie Body

1360 Holbrook Road, London E15 3AB.
E: anniebody@whyshouldiworkforyou.com T: 020 7946 0000 M: 077 0090 0000

At a glance
- Ex-Megabank Finance case officer with expert knowledge of pensions, financial crime and regulatory approval in the electronic money and retail sectors.
- Holder of a Financial Planning Certificate with more than 10 years' experience in finance-related roles.
- Seeking senior full-time/consultancy regulatory affairs/compliance engagements within financial services firms.
- Available for immediate incorporation.

Career summary
July 2007–present: Voluntary sabbatical (house renovation).
January 2000–July 2007: **Megabank Finance**. Roles included:
- Authorisations Department non-routine case officer. Assessing non-routine applications for authorisation against threshold conditions and making recommendations for approval or refusal. Worked closely with the Supervision, Intelligence and Enforcement areas, Regulatory Transactions Committee (RTC) and the Regulatory Decision Committee (RDC). Expertise in the retail sector, including electronic money issuers, plus experience of wholesale. Extensive knowledge of company handbooks and rules and how these are applied.
- Departmental financial crime representative. Assessing financial crime risks and responsibility for tackling financial crime issues, including staff training.
- Pensions review specialist. Providing guidance and support to the loss assessment outsourcers on calculation methodology, interpretation of procedures and general issues.
- Pensions review team coordinator. Heading a team of 12, dealing with investor affairs, signoff, technical meetings, performance issues and management information and statistics.
- Pensions review calculations signoff and calculation. Including investor liaison and coaching.

1998–2000: **Bigbank Life**. New business role assessing pension applications and liaising with independent financial advisers.
1998: **Nonesuch Employment**. Accounts administration, including pay and invoicing.
1997–1998: **Nondescript Recruitment**. Debt handling.
1996: **Banking Insurance Institute**. Administration.
1995: **Topbank Direct**. Insurance advice.

Qualifications
**Financial Planning Certificate** from the Chartered Insurance Institute.
**Master of Science** in Environmental Science from Wye College (University of London).
**Bachelor of Science** in Environmental Biology from Greenwich University, London.

Personal data
**Nationality:** British. **Languages:** Spanish (fluent). **Interests:** DIY (three property renovations to date), gardening, environmental affairs and music DJing (played at several bars and clubs in my younger years).

Spot the differences? Let's run through them.

1. **Length.** We've cut the CV down from two pages to one. Notice how having to lose half the information has almost doubled the impact of the CV. You are forced to really focus on the things that matter for the job, leaving out anything which 'is in there just in case' and which in fact is likely to distract, rather than attract, your prospective employer.

2. **At-a-glance**. This section is equivalent to the 'key skills' heading mentioned previously. Notice how it brings out all the really important things the employer needs to know. This section says: 'Here is why you should sit up and take notice. Now read on ...'

3. **Career summary**. Notice how this has been significantly tightened up so the prospective employer can take in all the details at a glance (plus this has provided room to include a few temp jobs with further relevant experience). In this case, the applicant's former job experience is very directly related to their future career role, so there is a lot of detail (about a third of the entire CV) on the last employer. Similarly, you will need to think carefully about which of your skills and experience are most relevant to the work you're interested in, and weight them accordingly.

4. **Qualifications.** Notice the old trick of just sticking to the three or four most notable qualifications? See how it actually makes the subject look smarter, not dumber, to mention fewer exams and grades? Plus it's a great way to hide not-so-outstanding school marks. We know, we know, it's a shame after all that effort you put into your GCSEs ...

5. **Personal data.** Here the 'interests' section has actually been beefed up a bit to help the candidate stand out from the crowd (note, after all, that this is someone going for a job in finance). A good rule of thumb for interests is: without being a complete liar, try to make yourself sound like the kind of person that your most interesting, sociable friends would want to have around for dinner.

**6. The rest.** Check and double-check your spelling and grammar! Did you notice that the word 'role' was incorrectly spelt 'roll' in the original CV? This is a howler that would not be picked up by a computer spell checker but would leap out at a literate employer. If you're not good at checking your own writing, get someone else to read through it for you. Actually, get someone else to read through it for you anyway. Their feedback could be invaluable. Note also that some thought has gone into the layout of the CV to make sure it can accommodate as much information as possible without becoming unreadable. Incidentally, the re-worked CV uses a typeface called Verdana which (along with Arial) is found on most computers and is particularly easy to read on screen.

*Tip: If you're intending to send out a lot of CVs by post, you might want to use a typeface such as Times which is easier to read on paper.*

### The key is in the words

Organisations that handle a lot of CVs, from online recruitment sites to large employers, increasingly store CVs in large databases and rely on search engines to pick out the ones that seem most suited to a particular job. This poses a slight problem: how are you going to wow an employer with your brilliant CV if you're not even sure they will get round to seeing it?

The answer is to make your CV attractive to search engines as well as to employers. And the way to do this is with keywords: words or phrases that the employer will use to find the applicants they need for a particular role. Coming up with a good list of keywords is not difficult, but does require a bit of imagination. Sit down with a piece of paper and try to think of all of the words you would use to describe the skills and responsibilities needed for your ideal role. Also think of the ways that role might be described, and the industry it's in. Try to picture yourself as the recruiter at a computer signed up to a CV search service … how will you be found?[35]

---

35. For advice on writing a brilliant online CV, visit www.jobsite.co.uk/onlinecvadvice.

## Searching for the answer

For example, if you're looking to find work in the charity sector, you might end up with a list of terms such as:

| | | |
|---|---|---|
| Action | Endowment | Poverty |
| Advocacy | Generous | Principles |
| Agency | Gift | Principled |
| Aid | Gifting | Public |
| Altruistic | Giving | Regulation |
| Assist | Good | Relief |
| Assistance | Grant | Rescue |
| Benefaction | Handicap | Responsibility |
| Benefit | Hardship | Rewarding |
| Benevolent | Help | Salvation |
| Body | Humane | Scheme |
| Care | Humanitarian | Service |
| Cause | International | Self-help |
| Charity | Non-profit | Travel |
| Charitable | NGO | Trouble |
| Community | NPO | Trust |
| Conditions | Organisation | Support |
| Contribution | Overseas | Voluntary |
| Cooperation | Philanthropy | Volunteer |
| Donation | Philanthropic | Welfare |
| Donations | Plan | Work |

(Note how a good thesaurus can come in handy for this exercise.) Now try to sprinkle these terms, or phrases that include them, liberally throughout your CV.

*Tip: Be careful about your keywords. Remember that you're in charge of the recruitment process, so you define what it is you're looking for. Do not include keywords for the sake of it. Look for words and phrases that reflect the kind of job you want to be in.*

### "Use active verbs where possible."

### Get active

Another trick, and not just for improving your chances of being found in a keyword search, is to use active verbs where possible. So, for example:

> *Don't say*: 'I was *the leader* of a team. '
> *Say*: 'I *led* a team.'

Most active verbs end in 'ed'. So try to load your CV with words ending in 'ed': achieved, chaired, consulted, coordinated, managed and so on.

---

**What NOT to do on your CV**
1. Lie.
2. List all the one-day training courses you have ever been on.
3. Include a passport photo.
4. Use swirly typefaces and bright colours to make your CV stand out.
5. Include sensitive information such as your passport number.
6. Start every sentence in the first person with 'I', 'My', and so on.
7. Use clichéd terms such as 'highly motivated individual', 'exceptional communication skills' or 'ability to work under pressure'.

---

# Getting it covered

So much for the CV. What about the covering letter and any other document-type paraphernalia you might need to secure a job? Well, as you might imagine, the rules for your CV apply equally well to anything else you're thinking of sending to an employer. So:
- Work out what really matters to the employer.
- Work out what you can offer that matches the employer's needs.
- Tell the employer about what you can offer as simply and succinctly as possible.

From then on it's all about showing passion in your covering letter, says Roslind Toynbee, a Career Coach from www.thecareercoach.co.uk. Here's how to excite an employer with your written word.

### Passion sells

Toynbee says: 'It is easy to revert to the same old clichés: 'please find enclosed my CV', 'I am writing to apply for the position of' and so on. In your opening paragraph you need to demonstrate knowledge and interest in the company you're applying to. Show that you have done your research and mention something about the company that you have read on their website, or, even better, in the trade press. For example: 'I noticed you won an award last week'.

'Use flattery and explain why you're excited by the company: it might be the award they have won, their reputation or commitment to excellence. Use phrasing such as: "I've been following your company in the trade press because I am excited by the pipeline project you've been working on".

### Show, don't tell

Put yourself in the shoes of the interviewer and ask yourself what your Unique Selling Point (USP) is. Use your second paragraph to list three key points that the company might want to know about you and that make you stand out. This could be your work experience; skills such as languages; then something that gives your letter personality. Perhaps you have a reputation for bringing in projects on time and on budget. If so, mention it here. Explain what opportunities you can help the company capitalise on, how you excel at problem-solving and how you can deliver for the company.

> *"Put yourself in the shoes of the interviewer and ask yourself what your Unique Selling Point (USP) is."*

# If you're unsure, use your contacts and phone the company beforehand to find out what's really important to them.

### Say it right

'Online applications can differ from written applications as many rely on computer scanning, so it's vital to include keywords and phrases that have been used in the original job advert,' says Toynbee. 'In the second paragraph, instead of the three bullet points detailed previously, you might list eight or nine skills using the exact words and phrases found in the job description with a brief explanation demonstrating how you possess them. In some applications you can even include a table, listing the role's requirements on the left side and what you can bring to the company on the right.

'Also, with written applications, be mindful that a junior HR person, who might not be familiar with industry jargon, could be doing the scanning, so, again, it's important to use some of the exact phrasing and key words from the job description.'

### Be provocative

In your final paragraph, don't be afraid to be bold and show that you're determined and passionate about the role. Never resort to the hackneyed phrase 'I look forward to hearing from you'. This is passive and weak. Instead use a positive sentence such as: 'May I call you in a week's time to check you received my letter and set up a meeting?', if you have applied speculatively for a position, or: 'May I call you in a week's time to check you received this and find out what the next steps are?' if you're responding to an advert.

### Looks matter

As a general rule, an 11-point font size should be sufficient in a standard font such as Arial or Times New Roman. Don't use coloured sheets or include photos. Good quality white paper and a laser printer is all you need. Get the layout right. Put your address in the top right corner; the employer's name, position, FULL address and date below, on the left. Always have a name to write to. If you're applying speculatively, make sure you phone up to see who will be receiving the letter.

After this, write the job reference number and/or the position you're applying for in bold and underlined. Covering letters generally get scanned in under 10 seconds, so you shouldn't need to write more than the three paragraphs outlined above. After all, you don't want to give away all the gold.

*"Covering letters generally get scanned in under 10 seconds."*

# Keep some examples back to talk about in the interview.

## THE RIGHT FORM

If the job you're after requires you to fill out an application form rather than send in a CV, don't worry. You may have to provide information about yourself in a more structured way (and according to a structure which suits your employer, not you), but that doesn't mean you cannot sell yourself.

If you want to create the best impression in an application form, remember to:
- Pay special attention to any sections where you're asked to expand on details of your employment history and/or qualifications. These are areas where you can highlight what it is that makes you the best candidate for the job. Copy the style you use for your CV.
- Try to fill out all the sections as much as possible.
- Write neatly if you're filling in a form by hand.
- Watch your spelling and grammar.

## OTHER DOCUMENTS

Does the role you're looking for require you to provide other types of written or printed material? Are you expected to show off a portfolio or showcase examples of your work? Then the same rules apply as before: don't throw in everything and the kitchen sink. Think carefully about the job you're applying for and select only the examples that best show off your most relevant skills. You can always provide other, less relevant samples later if the employer is interested.

# Bombarding your target with masses of irrelevant material will weaken, not strengthen, your case.

## TIME TO GET OUT THERE

Now you've identified the job(s) you want, built up a target list of employers, created a plan of attack and assembled an armoury of bullet-proof materials to sell yourself with. What happens next? Let's don our best interview suit and stroll calmly along to the next chapter to find out.

CHAPTER 7:

# Why you should hire me – part two

**What you'll get out of this chapter:**

- Ten tips from a top psychologist on what to do and what not to do in an interview.
- What to do if you suffer from stress … and what NOT to do in your first few seconds.
- Advice on dealing with phone interviews

THIS is it. After all the thinking, planning, researching, creating and marketing yourself towards a better working future, you got the call. The interview appointment. Now you're waiting, a little anxiously to be quite honest, in the reception area. Keep calm. Doesn't help that you were 10 minutes late, but at least you're here. A beaming minion darts towards you. 'Hi. Here for the interview? Follow me through here ….' As you stride purposefully into the meeting room, you fail to notice a chair leg sticking out in your way and seconds later you're sprawled across the floor, the contents of your briefcase and overcoat scattered around the room. What are your chances of recovering from this?

## PREPARATION IS CRITICAL

We will come back to this question in a minute, but first let us re-introduce you to David Moxon, the psychologist who you may remember put together the Happy Days test in chapter 1[36]. Here is what he has to say about interviews: 'It is all about preparation. People are confident when they're prepared. It's all about being in control.'

> *"People are confident when they're prepared. It's all about being in control."*

36. Not only that, but he has written two books – *Human Relationships,* Heinemann, ISBN-10 0435806548 and the unforgettable *Memory,* Heinemann, ISBN-10 0435806521 – and co-authored a third, *Psychology for AQA A: AS Student Book,* Heinemann, ISBN-10 0435806734

To make sure you do your best in the interview, says Moxon, it's worth learning as much as you can about the job and the company (here again is where your research will pay off), so you will not be caught off guard. It is also a good idea to come up with some stock answers to tricky questions.

*Tip: 'What is your greatest weakness?' is a question that often throws interviewees because the last thing you expect is to be asked about things you're not good at. But how about this for an answer: 'Probably my biggest weakness is I work too hard and sometimes do not get my work-life balance right ….' Be honest and not too clichéd; don't come out with 'I'm a perfectionist,' for instance. And say how you're correcting your weaknesses: 'My time management used to be poor but I'm reading a book on improving this and it's really helping me. I'm confident I will improve even further in this area very soon.'*

What else can you do to give the right impression? 'One thing we know is that smiling is really important,' says Moxon. 'People respond well to an open face. And no matter how hostile they look, try to make eye contact with them. If there is a panel, make eye contact with everyone on the panel.'

### PRIMACY AND RECENCY

Another thing you need to bear in mind are what Moxon calls primacy and recency effects; in other words, what you do first and what you do last in an interview. 'What you do first sets the scene but it's important how you leave as well', he says. To hit the right note in your interview:

1. Make sure your homework includes finding out what dress code is appropriate to the organisation you're visiting. 'Your appearance is initially the number one thing people will use to form an impression of you', says Moxon. 'We cannot all be Brad Pitt or Angelina Jolie, but you can make the most of your looks and enhance them. If you're going into a job that requires a suit and tie, wear them. Be appropriate. Generally, your dress code will be your opening gambit in the interview.'

*" Your dress code will be your opening gambit in the interview."*

2.  Leave your overcoat and bag or briefcase at reception so you're not caught trying to find somewhere to put them when you enter the interview room. And whatever you do, don't pull a list of questions out of your pocket. Says Moxon: If you cannot remember the basic two or three questions that you were going to ask about the organisation then you have a problem.

3.  Walk into the interview room confidently, shake hands with everyone there, make eye contact and smile. But don't overdo it. You do not want to appear so domineering that you're going to take control of the room.

4.  Be honest with your answers and back up your answers with facts and evidence where possible.

5.  Be careful how you speak. If you have a broad regional accent you might have trouble disguising it, nor should you try. But, says Moxon: 'There is always a tendency to speak fast. Slow down your speech a bit and it will help.' However, he adds, speaking fast at times can indicate excitement and passion, so do not slow down *all* your delivery.

6.  If someone on a panel does not seem interested in your answers then focus on the other interviewers to get a good reaction.

7.  Some interviewers will be quite tough with their questioning during interviews. You don't want to come over as spineless in these situations, but do not get into confrontation, either. If you have a strong view and can back it up, then do so calmly.

8.  Unless you're very familiar with 'tricks' such as neuro-linguistic programming, do not try using them. 'If I was on a panel and an interviewee started mirroring me I'd just get really annoyed,' says Moxon.

9.  Remember that you have the power. 'As a candidate you need to feel that this isn't a power game,' says Moxon. 'Your interviewer does not have the power. You have a right to be there. Just do not appear arrogant. Appear enthusiastic.'

10. Leave on a humorous note if you can, or at least in a confident manner and with a smile. 'How you leave is really important', Moxon notes. 'It is the last thing people will remember you by.'

> *"Leave on a humorous note if you can."*

## LESS THAN ZERO

And what happens if you trip up and fall flat on your face on the way in? Moxon: 'Bearing in mind that when you walk into the room you're basically starting from zero, if something terrible happens then within 15 seconds you could find yourself at, say, minus six in terms of your interviewer's attitude towards you.

'No matter how hard you back-peddle afterwards, you're still going to have to work hard to pull yourself back to zero, which is where all the other candidates started from. If you've made a really bad first impression, you may have to just put it down to experience.'

> Bear in mind that it isn't always in your power to turn an interview around. A lot depends on your interviewer(s) and what they're looking for. They may simply not click with you as much as they do with another candidate. (And if there is a potential personality clash between you and your prospective boss, you may be better off not getting the job.) By the same token, if you appear to have the kind of qualities your interviewer is looking for they may be much more forgiving of any slip-ups on your part.

## THINK BEFORE YOU LEAP

It is probably evident from the above that preparation, as mentioned earlier, is all-important. Think through the interview process. Dress appropriately. Imagine likely questions. Decide how you will deal with tricky ones. (And don't panic: we've got some help coming up on that in a minute.) Fail to plan and, that's right, you will plan to fail. Put some thought and effort into the process and you can vastly improve your chances.

Planning is also vitally important in helping you to avoid a serious interview problem that we all suffer from time to time: stress. If you become flustered in an interview then you're only a step or two away from a fully-fledged fight-or-flight response. Your heartbeat and breathing will speed up. Your guts will shrink. You may get tunnel vision and stop hearing things properly. You almost certainly won't perform well in the interview.

If you're someone who is easily stressed in interview situations, dress coolly and try breathing deeply or drinking some water if you start feeling nervous. Remember that you're in control of the situation and *this is just a job*.

*"Dress coolly and try breathing deeply or drinking some water if you start feeling nervous."*

## DEALING WITH PHONE INTERVIEWS

In the not-unheard-of event that you're given a phone interview, perhaps as a preliminary step in the recruitment process or because the employer is based overseas, you're in luck. Now you don't have to worry about what to wear. You don't have to worry about the fact that a spot the size of Mount Vesuvius has just appeared on your forehead. And you don't have to worry about memorising every last detail about your prospective employer. You can, and should, have notes to hand and refer to them when necessary. It also goes without saying that you should try as far as possible to minimise background noise and interruptions.

The downside of a phone interview is that it's unlikely you will be given a job purely on the strength of one. But even if it's likely to be followed by a face-to-face meeting, then at least it gives you and your potential employer a chance to assess each other, and perhaps begin building a rapport.

*Tip: In both phone and face-to-face interviews, beware of talking too much. It is important to listen to what you're being asked and then answer that particular question only. Try to keep your answers to less than four minutes. When you limit your time, you will tend to stay more focused. It is very easy to stray off the subject and ramble about things that are irrelevant to the job if your answer is too long.*

## WHAT ABOUT THE QUESTIONS?

Dressing the part, doing your preparation, creating the right impression … that's all well and good. But what about that inevitable question that comes out of left field and knocks your confidence for six? The one that leaves you spluttering and thinking 'now I've blown it'? How do you prepare for *that*? Easy! Just read the next chapter.

CHAPTER 8:

# Journey into the mind of the interviewer

### What you'll get out of this chapter:

■ Ten of the trickiest questions you could get asked at interview … and how to answer them.

■ A master class in interview technique from two top employers including their key interview questions.

■ How to avoid common pitfalls and always come out shining in your interview.

NOW, assuming you've dressed for the part, made it into the interview room without tripping up or otherwise embarrassing yourself, and are in a relatively calm and comfortable condition, there is really only one thing you need to worry about: giving the best possible answers to the interview questions. (Asking a few questions of your own is also important, but we'll come onto that in a minute.)

To help you with this, we figured it wouldn't hurt to turn to a couple of people who know a thing or two about employing people—and get them to give you a right grilling. Don't worry, though. Unlike the real thing, here your interviewers will tell you what they want to hear from you. These are just two of the employers who have lent their time and experience to an invaluable job hunting tool called Be My Interviewer, which you can find at www.bemyinterviewer.co.uk. Let's see what they have to say.

## FROM THE HEAD OF EGG

First up, step into our virtual interview room and shake hands enthusiastically with Mike Harris (don't forget to give him a big smile, too). In the last 21 years Harris has created four new businesses, including the internet bank Egg. Right now he is the chairman of a technology company called Garlik which started in 2005 and is expanding rapidly. He is also the chairman of Group Innovation at one of the biggest companies in the world, the Royal Bank of Scotland. So when it comes to spotting talented recruits, you can be sure that Harris knows his onions. (Or at least his Garlik. And his Egg.)

He says: 'You look for slightly different things if you're hiring for small start-up companies than if you're recruiting for a large company, but for me the fundamental principles are the same. Is the person I'm interviewing going to add to the talent and energy of the team they're joining? Or are they going to subtract from it? Will they fit in with the team? Will they fit in with the culture of the company? Will the skills and experience they bring fit what we need, when we're looking to fill this job?'

*"Is the person I'm interviewing going to add to the talent and energy of the team?"*

# What follows is a selection of Harris' favourite interview questions… and his tips on how he would want you to respond.

### Harris' question 1: Why are you here?
Harris: 'That question is deliberately slightly ambiguous. A little bit challenging. I'm looking to see exactly what sort of response I get. Now, obviously, an ideal answer at this point is somebody telling me what it is about the company which interests them, what it is about the job that interests them and why the experience they've had to date and the qualifications they've got make them a perfect fit for the job. If they don't come out with all of those right off the bat, that's fine. I can get that with follow-up questions. But it interests me where they start.

'Many people start by saying why their current job isn't working for them. I'd say that's not a great idea. When most people are looking for a new job, they'll have a positive reason or a negative reason for coming along. Positive reasons include being attracted to the job or attracted to the company.

Negative reasons are that something's not working, or they've got bored with their current company. I know both are in play but when they start I'd rather they accentuated the positives.'

### Harris' question 2: What are you passionate about?

Harris: 'Now this is my killer question. It really distinguishes people for me. It's a surprising question. People don't expect it. They don't expect to get asked that at work, or in a job interview. But for me, enthusiasm and passion are critical, particularly if I'm interviewing for a small company. Enthusiasm and passion are two of the few things that a small company has got as a competitive weapon against larger companies. Now I don't necessarily expect the person I'm interviewing to be able to infect other people with their own enthusiasm; that's the job of the leader. But I do want them to respond to somebody else's enthusiasm, to show me that they're capable of being enthusiastic and passionate about something.

*"Enthusiasm and passion are two of the few things that a small company has got as a competitive weapon against larger companies."*

'When I get an answer to this, often people will start off by picking a hobby, a sport, even their family. That's fine, but I normally follow it up with: "Tell me about something you could be passionate about at work." And if they can't come up with anything then, by the time I've warmed them up a little bit to the whole concept, then I'm suspicious.'

*Tip: Show your interviewer that there is something that gets you excited and enthusiastic at work. There's got to be something, or else why would you be bothering later on to ask 'Why should I work for you?'*

### Harris' question 3: What are the high points of your CV?

Harris: 'The two key words in that question are "high points". That question is not an invitation to spend 15 minutes going line by line through a CV. That doesn't impress anybody and I'm likely to stop somebody very quickly if they do it. Pick the things that are relevant and important. If you can do it in a minute, great. But certainly don't take more than two minutes. Pick the things you're most proud of, the things that are most relevant, the things that are most likely to impress the interviewer.'

### Harris' question 4: How did you get on with your last boss?

Harris: 'Bit of a trick question, that one. Ninety-nine per cent of people say: "fine". Then you get the obvious follow up, which is: "Come on, it can't have all been fine! What went wrong?" And to be honest, what you're just looking for here is for somebody to give you a pretty balanced view. Not everybody gets on perfectly with their boss, but what you really want to hear is: "It was fine, we got on fine. We developed a decent working relationship. Some things worked perfectly and some things didn't."'

### Harris' question 5: What do you look for in a person you're working for?

Harris: 'This is an opportunity for the interviewer to get a sense of what you need in your boss. For me, the perfect answer at this point is: "What I look for is that they give me enough space to do the job and when I need help I can ask for it and they provide it."'

### Harris' question 6: Can you tell me about a team you worked in that did a particularly good job?

Harris: 'Most good things in business are accomplished by teams. What I'm trying to get at in this question is some sense of how you're going to fit into a team. Are you going to be a team player? Or are you really not that sort of person? If you can tell me about a team that did a great job, I can follow it up with questions about what made it good, what your role was in the team, how the team worked, what the dynamics were like and so on. I'm very suspicious of people who can't talk about that stuff. I think: "Hmm, I doubt if they're going to be a good team player."'

### Harris' question 7: What can you tell me about anyone you admire?

Harris: 'I'm looking for two things in the answer to this question. Firstly I'm trying to weed out the cynics. Cynics never admire anybody. The cynics are a poisonous part of any organisation. You definitely

*"Cynics are a poisonous part of any organisation. You definitely don't want to recruit them."*

don't want to recruit them. So you want to come up with somebody you admire.

'But the second thing I'm trying to get a sense of is your values, by the sort of person that you admire.'

# What I would recommend, if you get asked this question, is to steer clear of politics. It can just be a little bit dangerous.

'Pick someone in your area of expertise. So if you're in technology, you could say Steve Jobs or somebody like that. Or somebody I've never heard of, somebody you worked with. And then you could say why you admired them, what it was about them that made you admire them. That will give me everything I need.'

### Harris' question 8: What are you really good at?
Harris: 'This should be a really easy question. It's an opportunity to make a powerful pitch about what you're good at, exactly what was asked for. And yet time and again I find that people are inhibited about making that pitch. This is not the time for false modesty. Go for it.'

### Harris' question 9: What areas of your work do you think need most development?
Harris: 'This is a polite way of asking for your weaknesses. Again, I find a lot of people are inhibited in saying what they're not so good at, but really we've all got faults. All I'm looking for there is just a little bit of honesty. Tell me what you're not great at. You don't have to be great at everything.'

### Harris' question 10: What makes you angry?
Harris: 'I'm looking for *something* here. Something always makes people angry. If people never get angry there is something lacking in them. But

here's an opportunity to give a really light hearted answer, you don't want to get too aggressive on this.'

*Tip: If you're asked this question, pick anything that does genuinely make you angry, but show that you don't get angry that often, that you can deal with it, and you're not going to bring anger into the workplace.*

*"The way you approach getting your first job is probably going to tell me how you approach everything else."*

### Harris' question 11: How did you get your first job?
Harris: 'This is a deceptively simple question that tells me an awful lot. I'm looking really for a couple of things in the answer to this. One is how you approach a task; the way you approach getting your first job is probably going to tell me how you approach everything else. So there's not a right answer to it; I'm just interested in what you've got to say. Where I do get impressed is some evidence here of determination and persistence, because quite often getting a job requires those two. And if you can demonstrate that in your answer, that's great.'

### Harris' question 12: What would your colleagues say about you?
Harris: 'The most common answer I get to this is: "I've no idea". Then you start to push people a bit and you start to get things coming through. The idea here again is to try and gauge cultural fit. Are you going to fit into this team? Are you going to fit into this organisation? Everybody has positive and negative things that colleagues say about them. It's not rocket science: pick the positive.'

### Harris' question 13: What do you find most satisfying about your work?
Harris: 'In this question I'm looking for some evidence of thoughtfulness and some evidence that the person I'm interviewing has something of an enquiring mind. From my experience, certainly, satisfaction comes from that sort of thing. You don't just go through the motions, you're actually thinking about what you're doing. I don't really care what interviewees say in response to this question, as long as there is something that they find particularly satisfying. And if they can't find anything then I'm very suspicious.'

## Harris' question 14: What don't you enjoy about your job?

Harris: 'There's really only one wrong answer to this question, because if you say "I enjoy everything" then I'm not going to believe you. There is always something you don't enjoy, so that's the first thing here: it's a question to gauge your honesty above all else. The other thing I'm looking for here is something that you can't determine for yourself. I'm just trying to judge whether the job that I'm offering is really going to work for you. And you can't do that, so you don't know. You can only be honest at this point and let me follow it up. And then we can engage in a conversation about whether this place and this job is really the right one for you.'

*"If you say 'I enjoy everything' then I'm not going to believe you."*

## Harris' question 15: If you could have changed anything about your last company, what would you have changed and why?

Harris: 'This question for me is a little bit of a tie-breaker, because nine times out of ten I get "I don't know" or "I wouldn't have changed anything". But the odd person who comes up with something really stands out. It shows me two things. One is that they have given some thought to the way they do their work and two is that they're likely to be a source of ideas. If that's important to the job I'm interviewing for then I'm going to be impressed if they come up with something.'

## Harris' question 16: What's going on in your area of expertise that's interesting right now?

Harris: 'The answer to this question normally depends on the job that I'm interviewing for. But if it's a technical role, particularly in IT, then I really do want to get a sense that the person I'm interviewing is up to date, is keeping an eye on what's going on and can tell me at least something that is happening that interests them.'

# In most professional or technical areas you really want a sense that the person is plugged in to what's happening, keeping themselves up to date, prepared to talk about it.

'If I don't get an answer to this question then I'm extremely suspicious.'

### Harris' question 17: Can you tell me about when your work was criticised or a good idea rejected?

Harris: 'Nobody likes being criticised. Nobody likes having ideas rejected. It happens to all of us. Really what I'm looking for here is a sense that while you may not like it, you can deal with it without being too defensive and preferably demonstrate that you can learn from criticisms and from the reasons people will give you about why your ideas have been rejected.'

### Harris' question 18: What is the most satisfying thing that you have ever accomplished?

Harris: 'This is a great opportunity to demonstrate enthusiasm and show yourself at your very best. You can really pick anything here. A lot of people pick something from university when I ask this question. The thing to do is to really engage the interviewer with your own enthusiasm for something that you did that you found particularly satisfying.'

> *"Really engage the interviewer with your own enthusiasm for something that you did."*

### Harris' question 19: Tell me about a time you were under pressure at work; what happened?

Harris: This is a tough question. Everybody gets under pressure at work from time to time. I'm trying to get at how you deal with it and what sort of coping strategies you have. The best answer to give is to pick a real situation where it happened, admit that you felt under pressure, because we all do. The best strategy in coping with pressure, and you may as well give this answer, is that you step back for a while, recover your attention, and you get back into action when you're ready. You don't let yourself get burnt out.'

**Harris' question 20: Can you make my job easy? Make me want to hire you.**
Harris: 'This should be an easy question. I can't tell you how many times people aren't prepared to make a little pitch about themselves. It's crazy: going to an interview and not being prepared to give a 90-second to 2-minute pitch about why you're the best person for the job. It honestly rather depends on what job you're going for; I have a lot more tolerance for people going for technical roles who are not able to do this brilliantly. But you know, I have been trying to recruit a salesman in the past where they've struggled on this question, and really that's the end of the game for them. You've got to be able to sell yourself.'

# Now meet Ian Ruddy ...

How did it go with Harris? Feeling a bit more confident now you know what he was looking for? Well, just in case, let's try another interview-with-answers for good measure. This time your interviewer is Ian Ruddy, Head of Human Resources Operations at Telefónica O2 UK, the mobile phone company. Here are 18 of his top interview questions – and the answers he wants to hear.

**Ruddy's question 1: Can you tell me what you know about O2?**
Ruddy: 'I would be looking for people to understand, first of all, that we're part of a bigger communications company called Telefónica, which operates in 23 countries across the globe. And also we're more than just a mobile phone company. We're a communications company offering not only mobile phone technology but broadband and other business services to customers across the UK.'

**Ruddy's question 2: Can you tell me what you think we are looking for in the people we might employ in our business?**
Ruddy: 'What we're looking for in our business is people that can demonstrate a passion and commitment for excellence in customer service.

*"What we're looking for in our business is people that can demonstrate a passion and commitment for excellence in customer service."*

Who can demonstrate from previous experience that they've often gone the extra mile to provide for a great customer experience.'

**Ruddy's question 3: Give me an example of a previous achievement you had within business and why it made you proud.**
Ruddy: 'We're looking for examples of what you did, any obstacles you faced, how you overcame those obstacles. And, in particular, what was it about the achievement that made you feel proud and special?'

**Ruddy's question 4: Tell me about a time when you were measured to weekly or monthly targets.**
Ruddy: 'Tell us what those targets were. How did you perform against the targets? Do you know how you were measured and where you were not necessarily meeting the targets? And what you had to do to achieve those end targets.'

**Ruddy's question 5: Tell me about when you had to work as part of a team and what you had to do to make sure you were successful as part of that team.**
Ruddy: 'Tell us about what role you played in the team. How the team kept together. What was successful about the team. How did the team celebrate success? How did it deal with fear? And how you dealt with conflict in the team.'

**Ruddy's question 6: What do you think is the right culture that you would be successful in at work?**
Ruddy: 'We're looking for more about the context within which you had to operate. For you to explain what part of the culture of the previous organisations you've worked in where you feel you were most successful.'

**Ruddy's question 7: What words would best describe your personality?**
Ruddy: 'The words we're looking for are words that fit into our culture and how we operate. We are a culture that is open, bold, trusted and clear. And I will be looking for words or phrases that link into those cultural aspects.'

**Ruddy's question 8: Can you tell me about an experience or success you've had that motivated you, and why?**
Ruddy: 'We would be looking for a clear, demonstrated example of what motivates you, what pleases you, what energises you. And then we can take a view on how it links to the way we work and operate at O2.'

**Ruddy's question 9: What are your strengths and your development needs?**
Ruddy: 'The answer to the question really comes from you, because you're the one who's aware of your strengths and your development needs. But we'll take that information and assess it against what we're asking you to do at O2.'

*"You're the one who's aware of your strengths and your development needs. But we'll take that information and assess it against what we're asking you to do."*

**Ruddy's question 10: Give me an example of where you've had to work with other people in different circumstances.**
Ruddy: 'I would be looking for a clear demonstration of where you have worked with others, or even where you've had to work on your own to achieve an end result.'

**Ruddy's question 11: Can you give me an example of a previous role where you were really successful?**
Ruddy: 'I would be looking for a clear demonstration of where you have been successful, not only in one area but many areas. That will differentiate you from other candidates.'

**Ruddy's question 12: Why do you want to work for us?**
Ruddy: 'I would look for a clear understanding of the role which you have applied for. A clear understanding of what expectations we have of someone in that role. And a good understanding about O2, its business and what might be its short-term goals or its longer-term goals.'

**Ruddy's question 13: What do you do outside work? What do you enjoy? Any hobbies?**
Ruddy: 'The answer I would be looking for would be a little bit more insight

about you, whether or not you play team games or sports or socialise extensively. At O2 teamwork is pretty key. But it's a fun and lively environment.'

**Ruddy's question 14: If I was to ask your current work colleagues about you, what do you think they might say to me?**
Ruddy: 'Clearly your work colleagues will say some great things about you. But tell me some things that you're not so good at, or maybe things they are not so keen on about you.'

**Ruddy's question 15: Can you tell me about something that you have brought to a previous role or business?**
Ruddy: 'Demonstrate examples of something you have done. Not as part of a team, but something that you were personally responsible for. I'm looking to get indicators as to whether you are proud about it, whether it was passionate for you, and did it motivate you.'

*"I'm not looking for too much negative, but a lot of positive."*

**Ruddy's question 16: A customer wants to end their contract. What do you do?**
Ruddy: 'So you've just been provided with an excellent opportunity to deliver a fantastic customer experience and to turn that customer into a fan of O2. What would you do? The answer I'm looking for is that you need to understand quickly why the customer wishes to end their contract with O2. You need to understand more about the customer in terms of their wants and wishes. And with that customer insight I am confident you can turn them around, deliver a great experience and retain them as a very loyal customer of O2.'

**Ruddy's question 17: Can you tell me what's good and what's bad about your current employer?**
Ruddy: 'What I'm trying to understand is whether you know what's good about your employer. But also we are keen to ensure people in our team are loyal to O2. So I'm not looking for too much negative, but a lot of positive.'

**Ruddy's question 18: Tell me about when you had to deal with a very difficult customer. How did you put it right for the customer and for you?**

Ruddy: 'That's often about doing things that are fundamentally different. Where you've gone out of your way to help that customer. So the customer will come back again and buy that product again, or shop at your store again, or call you again, because they have had a great customer experience.'

## AND NOW FOR THE MASTER CLASS ...

Hopefully by now you should be feeling pretty confident that you can handle any question an employer is going to throw at you. Well then, let's put it to the test.

# We've asked ten major employers to each come up with one of their toughest interview questions. And here they are, just for you.

*Tip: Have a bash at these* without *reading the answers first. Then see how close your responses are to what the employers are looking for. Rehearse your answers in your head if necessary.*

### Killer question 1

*From Karen Hood, the Human Resources Director of Virgin Atlantic, who interviews and recruits for board-level directors:* 'Imagine you and I are in an elevator and you have just one minute to tell me why you are the best person for this job.'

Says Hood: 'You've only got a very short space of time to tell me why you're the best person for the job. It's a very challenging question, but if you can answer it well, it really will serve you well in an interview. Basically, what are the real benefits of you in doing the job? Or what are the benefits or value you add to the organisation in this role? A very arrogant person will just sell features, not benefits. They'll say: "Well of course you need to employ me, because I'm just wonderful." But that doesn't really tell you anything, does it? What *does* tell you things is: "Well, I will add benefit because what I'm good at is ...", or "I will add value to your organisation because I've done it before and here's an example ...".

> *"A very arrogant person will just sell features, not benefits."*

*Tip: If you can think about the most powerful, quickest way of really selling the benefits of 'you', and marketing 'you' as a brand, then you're sure to get the job.*

### Killer question 2
*From Duncan Bannatyne, one of Britain's highest profile serial entrepreneurs and businessmen, widely recognised for his part in the popular BBC programme* Dragons' Den: *'I've interviewed 20 people for this job. Why should I employ you?'*

Says Bannatyne: 'The answer to that question is not to be totally modest and not to be totally arrogant, but to tell me quite honestly why you think you are the best person for the job.'

### Killer question 3
*From Nick Band, chairman and founder of the Band & Brown Group, one of Britain's leading public relations agencies:* 'What will I discover if I check you out on Facebook?'

Says Band: 'I expect people who work for me to have a keen interest in the media, and particularly in social media. So I would expect them to have a profile on Facebook. But you have to be very careful: it is very easy for your Facebook to turn into your Disgracebook. You can reveal an awful lot about your personality on Facebook, so be very careful what you do and what you say.'

> *"It is very easy for your Facebook to turn into your Disgracebook."*

**Killer question 4**

*From John-Paul Cardew, the talent resourcing manager for Broadcast & Corporate at BSkyB (whom we'll hear more from later in this book):* 'Why us? Out of all the organisations you could have applied for, why this one?'

Says Cardew: 'This is all about the candidate really selling themselves to us in terms of personality and cultural fit, what's going to set you apart from the rest of the candidates that we've seen. It's key for us because we've come across so many people before who haven't really researched the company, don't really know what we do—this is about you setting yourself apart as to why BSkyB should offer you the position.'

**Killer question 5**

*From Ruth Badger, a British businesswoman with her own consultancy firm, probably best known as runner-up in the second series of TV's* The Apprentice: 'Tell me about your biggest success ... now tell me about your biggest failure.'

Says Badger: 'The reason I do this isn't really to listen to your biggest success or even your biggest failure, but to understand if you can identify your own weaknesses. I know my biggest failure. That's because I'm very aware of what I'm good at, but I'm also very aware of what I'm not, which means I'm always looking to improve myself. That is something an employer will want to know."

**Killer question 6**

*From Oliver Lewis-Barclay, managing director and founding partner of Hooper Galton, an independent advertising agency:* "Have you ever been fired? And if not, why not?'

*"Getting fired is a good thing, and more than once is fine."*

Says Lewis-Barclay: 'The management guru Tom Peters said that getting fired is a good thing, and more than once is fine. The point he was trying to make is that sometimes we have to risk glorious failure in pursuit of creativity, or to maintain our integrity. So this is a deliberately provocative question, and whilst many people will never have been fired, what I'm trying to get at is whether you're the sort of person who would put their head above the parapet.'

**Killer question 7**

*From Steve Parker, managing director of MediaVest, one of the country's leading media planning and buying agencies:* 'What's your perspective on the current marketplace and what should we be doing to be more successful in it?'

Says Parker: 'I really like this question because it demands that you've done your research on MediaVest and you're an expert in the marketplace, but also, critically that you've got a point of view on my business and also what would lead to greater success in this marketplace. I think you've got to be careful because you don't know more about my business than I do, but I've given you the opportunity to have a point of view on my business. So there's an interesting balance to strike here. I want to see confidence and I want to see a point of view, but I don't want to see arrogance and I don't want to be told how to run my business. I've given you an open question and an opportunity to challenge me on the performance of my business. So I think it's a great question and it's one that needs to be answered quite carefully.'

**Killer question 8**

*From Peter Leadbetter of the global accounting firm Ernst & Young (EY):* 'Ask me the question you really want to know about our company, not the question you think will impress me.'

Says Leadbetter: 'I think this is probably towards the end of the interview. I'm looking for you to recognise hopefully that we've built a relationship by then. And to use that to ask that honest question. To engage in a dialogue with me around: "What is the reality of EY?" "What are the downtimes as well as the uptimes?" I want to understand that you're prepared – you have the courage – to ask those questions. Because you need to be absolutely sure that you understand what it is you're getting into, and what we're going to ask of you. And that's a question that gives people the opportunity to really get at the nitty-gritty.'

*"You need to be absolutely sure that you understand what it is you're getting into."*

**Killer question 9**
*From Jacqueline Gold, the chief executive of Ann Summers and Knickerbox:*
'What is your salary expectation for this job?'

Says Gold: 'This is a tricky question, so it's a good idea to perhaps throw the question back to the interviewer. You could first of all say that you need more information about the job and its responsibilities. You could also ask what range has been budgeted for the position.'

**Killer question 10**
*From Moray Coulter, the production talent executive for the factual and entertainment departments of ITV Productions:* 'What are your big aims in life?'

Says Coulter: 'Be honest, tell us what you really think. You never know; maybe we can help you make it happen.'

## OVER TO YOU

How was that? Now you know what (and what not) to do or say throughout your interview. But remember this is not a one-way street. As much as you're selling yourself to an employer, you need to check they can sell themselves to you. To make sure you ask the right questions and get the deal you need, both during your interview and beyond, is the subject of the next chapter.

CHAPTER 9:
# The job you want

*What you'll get out of this chapter:*
- ■ *Four questions to help you find out whether a job you're being interviewed for will suit your personality.*
- ■ *Fifty things you might want to ask your interviewer.*
- ■ *Four questions to ask about pay.*

IN the last chapter we went through what you need to do to strike the right note in your interview. We've given you a thorough mock grilling from two experienced recruiters. So you shouldn't have any trouble standing on your own two feet, and standing out, when you face the real thing.

But your interview is not about getting a job at all costs. If you create the right impression in your interview you *could* end up with a job offer. However, after all the effort you have put into finding a better career deal, you need to be sure this job is the right one for you before you sign up for it. You need to have the answer to the question 'Why should I work for you?' How? Easy. Make sure you have *your* say and ask the questions *you* need answers to while you're being interviewed. Turn your interview into an opportunity for you to find out more about the job and the employer.

## YOU ASK THE QUESTIONS

Most employers will not mind this. On the contrary, they will probably appreciate you wanting to know more about the role you're applying for and the fact that you're making an honest appraisal of whether it will work for you. By asking for information you will come across as being more interested, engaged and motivated. So you will actually be improving your chances of shining in your interview by trying to get information out of your employer. In fact, if you don't ask questions your prospective employer

*"By asking for information you will come across as being more interested, engaged and motivated."*

may wonder if you've got enough brains or initiative to be worth hiring. But what should you ask?

Remember the Jobsite Personal Profile (Chapter 3). One of the handy things about this is that it gives you a starting point for working out whether the job you're applying for will actually meet your personal needs and aspirations. Based on the test, we have worked out a whole series of questions you should ask depending on your personality type. Here they are.

## BALANCER INTERVIEW QUESTIONS

As a Balancer you want a work environment where good personal relationships are thought to be important. You have a preference for social responsibility and an acceptable balance between work and your wider life.

To make sure a job is right for you, here are four essential questions you should ask of your employer:
- How are decisions made in my area of work?
- How would you respond if I need to leave early to collect my children or otherwise deal with a loved one?
- Do you prefer individual or team objectives?
- What do you do to improve the wider community?

What kind of responses are you looking for? In general:
- The greater the emphasis the employer places on group decision making, the more you will like working there.

- The more flexible the organisation is regarding wider personal needs, the more you will enjoy it.

- The greater the emphasis the employer places on team objectives, the more it will fit your personality.

- The greater the emphasis the organisation places upon the wider community, for instance through corporate social responsibility activities, the happier you will be there.

## BELIEVER INTERVIEW QUESTIONS

As a Believer you're markedly different from all the other job seeker types. You have very little fear of unemployment and you're simply energised by loving what you do. You'll only work in an organisation as long as it interests you and you're not afraid to sub-contract your skills rather than be full-time employed.

The questions you need to ask at your interview are:
- How will I be managed?
- Will I be able to set my own objectives?
- Will there be scope for team decision making?
- How do you motivate your staff?

Here are the responses you're looking for:
- You want management to be as hands-off as possible. If your employer is essentially giving you free rein to get on and do your job as you see fit, then great.

- You do not mind objectives as long as you set them rather than have them imposed on you. So you effectively set the scope of your work.

- You want to make your own decisions rather than have them made by a group.

- Hah! You are self motivated and your employer should expect you to motivate yourself. The more they emphasise external motivation, the less well you may fit.

## CONTENDER INTERVIEW QUESTIONS

As a Contender you want an organisation that encourages and rewards individual achievement. Plus you want the opportunity for personal advancement. To make sure that is what you get, ask your employer these questions:

- Do you prefer individual or group objectives?
- How do people advance up through the organisation?
- What is done to encourage individuals to come up with new options?
- What scope is there for plenty of overtime?

Here is what you want to hear from your interviewer:

- 'We prefer more emphasis on individual objectives.'
- 'We prefer a focus upon individual initiative and new ideas rather than "doing what is required".'
- 'We are an organisation that rewards creativity and innovation.'
- 'We can offer you overtime and other types of financial reward.'

## SUPPORTER INTERVIEW QUESTIONS

As a Supporter you want to work in an organisation that has an established hierarchy and clearly defined rules and procedures. You want the opportunity to work to given standards.

The four questions *you* should ask of your potential employer are:

- What do you think makes a good employee?
- What standards will you use to assess my performance?
- Will you give me individual performance objectives?
- What can you tell me about your induction procedure?

*"As a Supporter you want to work in an organisation that has an established hierarchy and clearly defined rules and procedures."*

Here is what you're looking for in your interviewer's responses:
- When they're telling you about what makes a good employee, the more the answer focuses on doing the right thing or what the job description is, the better the fit with your personality.
- You want to hear them say that they have clearly defined standards.
- You're not well suited to roles where you're expected to set your own objectives, so it's better if your interviewer says that these will be set for you.
- The more structured and detailed the induction process, the better.

## SURVIVOR INTERVIEW QUESTIONS

As a survivor, you want an organisation where rules are simple and easy to apply. Ask:
- How much time will I spend on paperwork?
- How much time will I be physically active?
- Do you set performance objectives that extend beyond a day, say weekly, monthly or annually?
- Will I work in teams that make decisions

This is what you want to hear:
- The less time on paperwork, the better.
- The more time on physical activity, the better.
- When objectives become increasingly long-term, you're less likely to be interested in the job.
- You're not interested in things like group decision making.

## FIFTY QUESTIONS FOR YOU TO ASK

In addition to the specific questions above, there are many other things you will probably want to find out about the job. How much you will be able to enquire about in practice will depend on the amount of time you have; after all, you need to allow the interviewer to do some questioning, too. You may find you get told a lot of the information you need before you are even asked if you have any questions.

*"You may find you get told a lot of the information you need before you are even asked if you have any questions."*

Here is a list of generic questions for you to bear in mind when deciding what to ask about in your interview:

1.  What are your organisation's strengths and weaknesses compared with your competitors?
2.  How important is this department or position within the organisation overall?
3.  What are your plans for the next two, five or ten years, and how does my role or department fit into them?
4.  What is the structure of the organisation or department?
5.  How will you measure my performance, who will do the measuring and how often?
6.  What will I be doing on a day-to-day basis?
7.  What sort of people do you usually look for?
8.  What skills and abilities would I need to succeed in this job?
9.  What is your policy on training and development?
10. What IT systems do you use?
11. What sorts of things am I likely to end up doing in my first year here?
12. What kind of work will I be doing? Is it mostly routine or does it change much day by day?
13. How much will you help me to achieve my career goals?
14. What kinds of responsibilities will I have on day one?
15. What would you consider to be an ideal employee?
16. What about foreign placements or travel abroad?
17. How big is your department and how much does it contribute financially to the organisation?
18. Does your organisation have plans for expansion?
19. How is your organisation responding to the current trends in the industry?
20. How would you describe your corporate culture and values?
21. How would you describe your management style?
22. What opportunities and threats does your organisation currently face?
23. What are my chances of promotion and how soon might I expect to move up?
24. What things do you prize in your team?
25. How well is your organisation doing within the industry?

26. How do people elsewhere in your organisation see your team or department?
27. What were your team or departmental goals last year, and did you meet them?
28. What are your current team or departmental goals? Who set them and do you think they're achievable?
29. What are your team or department's main challenges? What are you doing to solve them?
30. What do you think will be the greatest challenge for me in my job?
31. What do you think are the best things going for your team, department or organisation?
32. What do you expect me to achieve in this role?
33. How often will we have meetings and appraisals?
34. Which of my responsibilities will be the most important?
35. Are my responsibilities likely to change?
36. How much time do you think I will spend carrying out different aspects of my job?
37. What did my predecessor(s) achieve in this role?
38. What has happened to the people who worked in this role before me?
39. Why aren't you filling this position from within?
40. What would I have to have in order to do well in your organisation?
41. What can I get from you that I couldn't get from your competitors?
42. What do *you* like about working with this team or organisation?
43. Why did you select me for an interview over other candidates?
44. When will you be able to tell me whether or not you will be offering me a job?
45. If you make me an offer, when do you need me to get back to you with an answer?
46. What are my chances of rotating round to other jobs in the organisation?
47. Do you support vocational training and development, for example to help me complete a Masters in Business Administration?
48. What is likely to be my career or promotion path in this role?
49. Who else works in the team or department, and what are they like to work with?
50. What hours do you expect me to work? How flexible is this?

## HALF A DOZEN QUESTIONS FOR MANAGERIAL JOBS

If you're being interviewed for a manager's job, then here are a bunch of other questions you should ask:

- How many people will I be in charge of and what do they do?
- How much autonomy will I get in managing this team or department?
- Are there any people that I need to watch out for on the team?
- Are there plans to sack, hire or promote anyone?
- Are there any problems with motivation or morale that I should know about?
- What is the organisational structure I will be in charge of?

### SHOW ME THE MONEY

No matter what your personality profile or how little emphasis you place on earning lots of cash, at some point you're going to need, or want, to know how much you will be getting paid. For some people, pay can be a bit of a touchy subject. It shouldn't be.

*"For some people, pay can be a bit of a touchy subject. It shouldn't be."*

# If you have just spent 40 minutes going into the minutiae of what you can do for a potential employer, the least they can do is take 5 minutes for an honest and upfront discussion of what you will get in return.

*Tip: Leave pay discussions until the end of the interview so you can be certain that it's the kind of job you really want and have (hopefully) been able to create a positive impact. But no matter how well you have been getting on with your interviewer, don't leave the room without getting a good idea of what you will be paid. Otherwise, how are you going to work out whether the job is worth taking?*

**Four questions to ask about pay**
- Roughly what salary are you offering for this post?
- What other perks and benefits are there?
- How is my pay likely to change in the next few years?
- Do you offer commission or bonus payments? How much are they, usually?

## AFTER YOUR INTERVIEW

Once you've asked your questions and had a chat about pay and benefits, it's probably time to end the interview. Before you go, be sure to find out what the next step is – another interview or a job offer (or not), for example – plus when and how you will be told about it.

Remember to leave on a positive note. Offer a firm handshake and a broad smile. If this is a job you really like and you have got on really well, then you could be closing the deal. If you're not sure, you have still had some good interview practice and learnt enough about the employer to be able to cross them off your list.

## FOLLOWING UP

If you haven't heard back from the employer within a reasonable amount of time – a week, say – after your interview, there is no harm in calling or sending an email to their Human Resources or Personnel department to get an update. Keep the tone upbeat and optimistic: 'Keen to hear from you and is there anything else you need?' rather than 'Where's my job?' or 'Does this mean I haven't got it?' It's not unusual for recruitment to drag out, particularly in small organisations where people are more likely to become distracted by day-to-day issues.

By the same token, however, never pin all your hopes on one particular job. Stay in control of the recruitment process by following up other employment options. The more interviews you attend, the better your understanding will be of the things that employers in your market can offer you. This in turn gives you greater bargaining power when a job offer comes along.

Similarly, if you get offered a job which you're only marginally interested in, you can use it as a way of prompting a response from other organisations whom you may have met with: 'I have already got an offer on the table from one of your competitors but didn't want to accept it without first finding out whether you had a position for me ….'

> *"If you get offered a job which you're only marginally interested in, you can use it as a way of prompting a response from other organisations."*

## GETTING AN OFFER

If you have done your analysis, targeting and preparation properly, and managed to strike a chord during your interview, then sooner or later the chances are you will get a job offer for a role you really, really want to be in. But don't break open the bubbly just yet[37]. What you've been told at interview is one thing, but it pays to check your employment contract to make sure it's not another.

## SIX THINGS TO WATCH OUT FOR

Philip Landau, a member of the Employment Lawyers Association who represents employees as a partner and founding member of the law firm Landau Zeffertt Weir, says there are six main areas you need to watch out for in employment contracts.

1.  Notice periods. 'This could unduly hamper your mobility to move,' says Landau, 'especially if there is a long period of notice and your new employer is not minded to hang around waiting. A long period of notice is anything over six months. It is quite usual to have a period of three months but even this could be considered too long for a new employer to wait if you want to switch jobs. On the other hand, you may prefer the security of a longer notice period if, say, you were made redundant. In this case, a longer notice period will give you an extra financial cushion at the time when you might most need it.'

---

37. Oh all right, then. Maybe a glass or two. A job offer is a job offer after all. Well done.

The question you need to ask yourself is: in a worst-case scenario, am I likely to jump or be pushed? If the former, aim for a shorter notice period. If the latter, try to get a longer period.

2.  Look out for post-termination covenants restricting your ability to take clients, customers and other staff for a period of time after you leave employment. Usually the period is six months but it can easily be three or even 12. Such covenants may also restrict you from working for competitors. Again, says Landau: 'You need to gauge what you think you might want or need to do in a worst-case scenario.'

3.  Mobility clauses. 'Check that the contract doesn't allow your employer an unfettered discretion to move you within the country, or even abroad, if you aren't willing or able to relocate.'

4.  Bonuses. Check that any bonus clause is not too wide. Some guarantee is best, but many bonus clauses provide for an absolute discretion by the employer. 'The wider the discretion is, the less ability you have to challenge it,' Landau says.

5.  Make sure the role you're carrying out is properly set out in the contract. The looser this is, the easier it is for the employer to change your role. And it may not always be for the better.

6.  Check that your salary, benefits and holiday entitlement are all correct. Many employees can be surprised that they're not receiving the benefits they thought they were, simply by not checking their contracts at the outset.

*"Check that your salary, benefits and holiday entitlement are all correct."*

### Sticking to your guns

What things are worth fighting your corner over in an employment contract? Landau says: 'You should not back down on agreed remuneration, job title or holiday pay, or mobility if you really do not wish to work away from the base where you have been primarily offered to work at.

'You will probably have to end up compromising on bonus clauses and clauses relating to post-termination restrictions as employers usually like to apply consistency in this regard.'

No contract? No problem, says Philip Landau of Landau Zeffertt Weir solicitors. 'An employment contract is important. But you should remember that even if you do not sign one, you can still have a verbal contract where most of the terms will be implied from what happens in practice. You would still maintain all your employment law rights, with or without a written contract. And in any event you have the ability to apply to the employment tribunal for a written statement of your terms of employment. This is not a contract as such, but a statement of the basic terms.'

Notwithstanding this, it always helps to get as much as possible from your employer in writing, upfront. More of this later.

### Tighten up

In general, it's in your employer's interests to take you on with a job description that is as wide as possible. This means they can then pretty much ask you to do whatever they like within the terms of your contract. Move you to a location on the other side of the country, for instance. Or get you to take on twice as much responsibility for the same remuneration.

This is particularly the case the higher you go up the corporate food chain. To an extent you will need to resign yourself to the fact that if you're being paid more and given more responsibility then your employer has a right to ask more of you.

In addition, the extent to which you can dictate the terms of your work contract may be limited. Empowered employees who ask 'why should I work for you?' are still few and far between, and most employers expect you to be grateful to get any job, no matter what terms, especially if there are few jobs available at that time or in your region.

If you feel you have done a good job of standing out from the pack, however, and have been able to demonstrate that you could be a loyal, committed and happy employee, then it would not hurt to get clarification on any terms that you do not feel completely happy about. Contracts are often shrouded in legalese and there is no shame in admitting that you're not sure exactly what a particular clause means. Similarly, employers may hand you a standard work contract containing points that do not apply to you or your role.

*Tip: Don't be pernickety when it comes to the terms of your employment contract. And be realistic about how much you might be able to get a contract changed in your favour. But do make sure you understand what you're getting yourself into. Query any terms you're not sure about. Be prepared to stand your ground on any points which are of major importance to you. Handle your contract negotiations in a no-nonsense, professional way. It will help set the tone for the rest of your employment.*

## WAVE GOODBYE TO YOUR OLD JOB

In 2006, Steve Moseley, a car salesman in Fareham, Hampshire, told his boss to 'stick his job' after scoring what he thought was a million-pound win on a lottery scratch card. His elation was short-lived, however. Twenty minutes later he realised he had mis-read the numbers and had to ask for his job back. Several times. Soon after, he left the company[38].

---

38. As reported online by the BBC. See 'Lottery blunder for car salesman', at http://news.bbc.co.uk/2/hi/uk_news/england/hampshire/6209462.stm.

Mr Moseley's mishap is a good illustration of why it's always worth making an effort to leave your current employer on good terms, no matter what the circumstances. You have no way of foretelling what will happen after you leave. And while hopefully you will not be reduced to begging for your old job back, you may need to ask your current boss to give you a reference in the future. So make it an amicable parting of ways. Who knows, your old boss may even end up being a cherished client in the future[39].

> *"It's always worth making an effort to leave your current employer on good terms."*

## The fine art of resigning

Kate McCarthy, managing director of McCarthy Recruitment, is an expert on how to resign in a professional manner. And it pays to plan ahead, she says.

'Accepting a new position is an exciting time,' she points out. 'Looking forward to your future career can and should give you a real sense of achievement. However, before you can move on you have to leave the job you're currently in and handing in your resignation can be a daunting prospect.'

Too true. So here are some guidelines covering what to do and what to say to help you resign in a professional manner.

### *Timing your resignation*

Resignation needs a lot of careful thought and preparation. If it's handled in the right way it will demonstrate a positive and mature personal approach to your decision. Alternatively, if you approach it inappropriately and awkwardly, negative feelings and recriminations can occur and these could affect your career in the future.

Think about your boss and your work patterns and decide when you're going to resign. For example, a Monday morning may not be the best option. Ask to sit down in a private office and ensure you're away from the shop floor or your department.

---

39. Take a look at www.jobsite.co.uk/podcasts for some advice from Ian Ruddy, whom we met earlier, on leaving your old employer gracefully.

### The meeting

Resignation is a sensitive issue and it may be difficult to predict the outcome of such a meeting to discuss it. So preparation is critical. Your boss may well congratulate you. Or they may equally feel betrayed and you could even find yourself in a conflict situation. So expect the unexpected, plan ahead the best you can and follow the golden rule of remaining professional at all times. Here are some more points to help you prepare for your meeting:

- Plan what you're going to say and stick to it. Be firm yet polite. You have not made this decision without serious consideration. If you walk into the office to resign and you leave agreeing to stay you will in most cases have eroded the respect that your boss had for you anyway.

- Retain your composure at all times and ensure that you can articulate why you're leaving, focusing on the positives of your career move. You will not gain anything by using the meeting to dwell on negatives. Remember that you may need a reference from your boss and there could be a time in the future when you meet again. So always be professional and try to set aside your emotions. That way you will remain focused on resigning rather than on justifying your decision.

*"Remember that you may need a reference from your boss and there could be a time in the future when you meet again."*

- The meeting does not have to be lengthy and although you will no doubt be questioned about your reasons for leaving, you do not have to offer detailed answers. Remember what you have decided to say. And don't deviate from your intentions.

- Ensure that you have thought through the notice period you're prepared to give. Stress that you will provide a detailed handover. And where possible, reduce your notice period to an agreed timescale.

- Be prepared for a counter offer. And when it comes, be ready to reinforce the fact that you would like them to respect your decision.

■ Leave the meeting on a positive and amicable note, with an agreement for your leaving date.

### Managing a counter offer

Once upon a time, you handed in your notice and looked forward to your leaving party. It's not quite that simple anymore. Today when you resign, you may be given a counter offer. But beware, after the initial flattery and extra cash have lost their appeal, you may still be left feeling exactly as you did when you started looking for a new job.

Furthermore, a counter offer that improves your financial package can simply mean that you receive your standard pay rise early, so it could lead to disappointment later in the year. Plus, once you have handed in your resignation, your loyalty and commitment may be called into question, and as a consequence, you may find yourself being passed over for promotion. So accepting a counter offer can seriously damage your job prospects. Even when the counter offer includes the promise of promotion, it may still never materialise. And unless you have it in writing, you will be left high and dry.

The facts speak for themselves. A counter offer is often the most cost-effective and productive solution to your resignation. Persuading you to stay may be cheaper than recruiting your replacement. So for your employer, it may not be all about you. It's sound economics.

*Tip: If you find yourself being tempted, remember that national statistics show 89% of all employees who accept a counter offer leave within the next six months.*

## WHY SHOULD I EMPLOY YOU?

That's almost it. Worked out what you need to make you happy. Looked for employers that can provide it. Wooed them with a flashy CV and a flawless interview technique. Checked you're happy with the small print of your job offer. And left your no-good old job. All that is really left now is to get your new career off to a flying start and make sure it stays on track from now until your retirement. We'll deal with this later on. But first let's take a brief detour into the heart of employer territory. And let's find out why it is that they would be willing to put up with you asking 'Why should I work for you?' in the first place.

CHAPTER 10:
# The corporate view

*What you'll get out of this chapter*:
■ *Understanding what you could get if you worked for one of the country's top employers.*
■ *Learn why you are attractive to leading employers.*
■ *Tips on how to be the person they need to have.*

TRY telling Scott McNaughton it's a boring life being an accountant. In 2005, at the age of 31, he became the youngest partner at BDO Stoy Hayward, the UK member firm of BDO, the world's fifth-largest accountancy organisation. The firm promptly agreed to let him have time off from work to scale Aconcagua, the tallest mountain in the Southern hemisphere and the highest peak outside the Andes, which he did on New Year's Eve in 2005.

Pretty impressive, maybe. But not enough for McNaughton, who went on to climb Mount Everest the following year as part of a £20,000 fundraising effort. Once he had organised time off and discussed what the experience would allow him to bring back to the firm in terms of personal development, BDO Stoy Hayward contributed to his sponsorship.

## A WILLING SPONSOR

In 2007, McNaughton swapped the mountain slopes for the open sea in what has been described as 'the toughest endurance event on earth': crossing from Europe to America in a two-man rowboat as part of a contest called the Woodvale Challenge Atlantic Rowing Race. The route from La Gomera in the Canary Islands to Antigua in the West Indies took 69 days and aimed to raise £20,000 for the charity Diabetes UK. This time it was a bigger hurdle to obtain time off. However, the firm appreciated the benefits that Scott's experience would bring and ultimately was very supportive, giving him a significant amount of unpaid leave.

*"The firm appreciated the benefits that Scott's experience would bring."*

'I've been tremendously fortunate in being able to work for a firm with which I could have a sensible conversation on the returned benefits for these sorts of activities, and that believes in helping its people to excel, both at work and in their lives in general,' says McNaughton. 'I would never have been able to do the things I have done without the support of the business.'

McNaughton is quick to point out that the challenges he has to deal with at work can be every bit as taxing as those he sees in his outdoor adventures. As a rising star in a busy international advisory firm, he wrestles daily with high finance issues facing major British companies in advertising, retail, technology and other fast-paced industries. This often involves drawing on past experiences and coping with high levels of pressure, something his external activities have helped with. 'I work very hard to help the firm be successful and ensure value is put back into the business. That is why the business has helped me to be successful in my personal pursuits,' he says.

### Portrait of a top employer
Clearly, McNaughton works for an organisation which is able to give a pretty good answer to the question: 'Why should I work for you?' But how common are these organisations? How easy is it to get into them? And why are they prepared to place such an emphasis on employees in the first place? Taking the last question first, let's look again at BDO Stoy Hayward[40].

The firm may not always have been seen as an exceptional employer. At the beginning of the century it would pretty much have rated no better or no worse than any other accountancy business in terms of its employment practices.

### The value of values
But by about 2002 the business was keen to grow and was facing similar challenges to other firms in recruiting people in a tight market. Larger firms were able to attract graduates more easily by virtue of being more well-known brands.

---

40. In the interests of full disclosure, it should be noted that one of us has been a long-standing adviser to BDO.

At the same time, BDO Stoy Hayward, which had recently undergone a process of consolidation of a number of separate firms, spent a fair amount of time looking into what its core values were and should be.

The values of an organisation are something like a definition of its culture. They are the things that make it tick and that it strives towards in its everyday operations. BDO Stoy Hayward identified four: strong and personal client relationships, honesty and integrity, mutual support, and taking personal responsibility.

*Tip: When you come to search for an employer that you would like to work for, pay attention to any values or mission statements they might have. These should give you a pointer as to how the organisation sees itself. And keep an eye open, too, to see if the people in the organisation seem to live up to its values when you meet them.*

### An employer of standing

Having, in a sense, defined the culture of the organisation, the partnership decided to see if it could improve its standing as an employer in order to attract the people it needed for its ambitious growth targets. The trick was not to throw money at the problem and just offer better salaries. After all, despite its size the business could easily be financially outgunned by the so-called Big Four major accountancy firms that were its main competitors. Instead, the business wanted to show that it was a place where people could be individuals, where lives as well as work would be valued, and where employees would never feel like a cog in a big wheel.

### Taking the corporate pulse

'We have an annual employee survey called Pulse which we used to find out what it was that we were missing,' says Irena Molloy, head of human resources at BDO Stoy Hayward.

'We used it as the basis for making changes to the business, addressing the areas where we were scoring badly against external benchmarks.'

BDO Stoy Hayward enhanced its pay structure, pensions and benefits and made a big deal of the fact that it was willing to listen to its employees. It provided a wide-ranging flexible benefits scheme. Provided lifestyle-related services such as free mortgage advice. Made it easier for people to work flexibly. In an industry dominated by numbers, Molloy says: 'We began to be seen as a place where you were recognisable as an individual.'

*"A place where you were recognisable as an individual."*

In fact, the recognition went far beyond individuals. In 2004, the firm was named Employer of the Year by the industry magazine *Accountancy Age*. This was quite a feat since the award was dependent on votes from employees themselves. But BDO Stoy Hayward did it again the next year. In 2005, the firm entered *The Sunday Times'* Best 100 Companies to Work For listing and the following year was at number 19 on the list.

### Employer awards

In 2007 it gained another *Accountancy Age* Employer of the Year award, as well as being listed as one of the United Kingdom's top 50 workplaces by the *Financial Times*. By 2008, it was becoming a regular fixture in the *Financial Times* and *The Sunday Times* lists and at the time of writing was, safe to say, easily the most widely recognised employer in the accountancy sector.

Something else happened to BDO Stoy Hayward during this period. It grew faster than any other major accountancy business in the country. And while it's difficult to draw a direct link between employee satisfaction and business growth, the fact remains that BDO Stoy Hayward's excellent employer credentials helped it to attract enough new employees to handle its expansion.

Says Molloy: 'We've been very successful in our graduate recruitment, which is a huge part of our intake. We've had really good people come to us and choose us over the Big Four. Anecdotal evidence points to candidates and current employees being impressed with the values and flexibility of the business, and this was reflected in our awards. Our retention of key staff was high.'

## Successful recruitment

Molloy is cautious about reading too much into the impact of employment practices on BDO Stoy Hayward's business success. The firm has little data to support a cause-and-effect linkage between employee satisfaction and profitability. Plus there are other market factors that could go some way towards explaining BDO Stoy Hayward's growth, such as the fact that it is well positioned to exploit conflicts of interest between the Big Four firms serving large corporate clients. Nevertheless, in some respects it's only commonsense to assume that having a contented employee base will be beneficial to the employer.

'There's no doubt that if you've an engaged, happy and motivated workforce, sickness absence is reduced,' Molloy says.

## REWARD STAFF, REAP BENEFITS

This sentiment tallies with the experience of other employers. Sally Cohen, who is managing director of the cosmetics company Elizabeth Arden (UK), says: 'Recently we did an engagement study and we really did find that people who are very involved, feeling they can really make a difference, did want to stay and were more likely to be happy, productive employees. Engagement and commitment are the highest predictors of whether people will stay at the company. Happy employees are almost always more productive.'

At the drinks maker Diageo, human resources business partner Kevin Bohan agrees. 'The higher our engagement scores, the better an environment we are creating for our people, which in turn leads to higher team and individual performance,' he says.

## The lengths employers go to

Like BDO Stoy Hayward, these employers go to great lengths to keep staff happy, loyal and productive. At Diageo, where job perks include an exclusive in-house cocktail bar[41], 'We run a workplace culture survey where we ask people how we are doing as a company versus a set of values and a universally defined set of engagement questions,' says Bohan.

41. For the record, Diageo is also fully committed to promoting responsible drinking, with a strict code of practice on the subject.

Diageo's motto is 'celebrating life, everyday everywhere', no less. Bohan says the company strives to make sure it does this on a daily basis, from the minute people walk in the door: 'It is more than a basic form of celebration; it's a way to inspire and give meaning to the work we do.'

The generic questions that the company asks its employees in its workplace culture survey include whether it is a great place to work and whether bosses are supportive of professional and personal growth. 'We take it seriously and are always looking at how we can make Diageo a better place to work, thus improving our performance and improving the scores,' Bohan notes.

### A partnership with the individual

In addition, he says: 'At Diageo, each individual owns their career. It's a partnership between the individual, their manager and Diageo. We provide the tools and processes to help them steer their

*"At Diageo, each individual owns their career."*

careers. This includes a framework for them to understand the capabilities needed for each job or to help them understand their aspirations. We also help managers, telling them "here is what you can do to help your employees get where they want to go". This includes more flexible working options, so people can work from home and use new technologies to help them do so.'

Elizabeth Arden also places great emphasis on flexible working. 'We recognise the need for a work-life balance,' says Sally Cohen. 'It's one thing to talk about it, but another to make it happen, for example to be flexible if people want to work four-day weeks or work remotely. We do that; we recognise that people have lives beyond work. And that recognition makes them better employees and that makes them more productive and happy. We do this for all levels. Flexibility in career paths is important, too. We might hire you in sales but we can move you around, to marketing for example. Or from a back office job to front-line sales.'

*It ain't all about cash*
There are good reasons why hard-nosed business organisations should invest in touchy-feely employment practices. The most obvious is the

fact that happy staff tend to be more motivated and hard-working. But another very significant point is that treating its employees as human beings can actually save business money in the long run. As was the case with BDO Stoy Hayward, giving people more flexible working hours, better training and promotion opportunities or other fringe benefits can help an organisation attract employees even when it's not offering the best pay packet in the sector.

*"Fringe benefits can help an organisation attract employees even when it's not offering the best pay."*

Kevin Bohan says: 'Partly what makes a top employer is providing reward packages at the top end of its category in order to attract the best people, though this is not always the case. A top company in the United States, for example, is known as an amazing place to work for even though its compensation is at the lower end of the top remuneration for its sector. It's such a fun place to work, with such a good environment, and people enjoy working there so much the company doesn't have to pay the very highest salaries to attract and retain them.'

These employers have realised that if an employee asks 'Why should I work for you?', the answer will not always be 'Because of the cash'.

*What makes a top employer?*
What things can you look out for in order to tell whether a prospective employer cares about its people? Here are some indicators:

- It takes care of you and has a paternalistic approach to employees.
- It makes sure you will grow professionally, providing plenty of development opportunities but also pushing you to improve.
- It is recognised in the marketplace and there are certain expectations of what it will be like to work there.

■ It attracts high-calibre recruits from other organisations, so you can be sure you will be working with talented people.

**Case study: the Sky is the limit**
John Paul Cardew's title says it all, really. At Sky, the communication and entertainment broadcaster, he is the talent resourcing manager for corporate and broadcast. So it's already pretty clear this is a company which doesn't see its people as a mere 'human resource'. Having a brand which reaches daily into nine million households is a big responsibility, says Cardew, and one which the company takes seriously by rigorously selecting each of its 14,000 or so employees.

Sky is very much on the frontline of the war for talent, says Cardew. 'We are a lot of people's first choice for when they switch on the TV, PC or mobile phone. So we get a large number of applications for things like making programmes or working behind the camera. These applications sometimes include show reels, each of which we review. We're looking for creative and passionate people, who fit in with our values: irrepressible, inviting, tuned in and fun.'

*Fighting the war for talent*
The company looks for similar attributes in people destined for other areas of the business, such as marketing or finance. However, offering a fantastic brand may not always be enough. Cardew notes: 'You cannot rest on your laurels. We give people a challenging work environment, not in terms of long hours but in terms of using your brain. It's also quite an entrepreneurial environment. We listen to ideas.'

*"Offering a fantastic brand may not always be enough."*

In return for hard work and creativity, Sky employees get rewards not just for themselves but also for their partners and families. Sky's package includes private healthcare, a competitive pension plan, offers on computers and bicycles and the Sky Christmas Stocking, a grab-bag of goodies from which staff can select their own yuletide gift, such as a day out or tickets to the theatre. Plus there is Skyfest, a two-day summer extravaganza for employees and their families where entertainment is laid on by the company's own pool of television talent.

Cardew believes Sky's people are worth the effort: 'If you don't look after your staff you'll lose them. You've got to be able to work in an environment that is inviting, and fun at times. Why? Because we want what you see in front of the camera to be the best product out there. And to put that out we need the best people working on it. That goes from the chief executive to the chef making lunches in the canteen.'

## SNARING A TOP EMPLOYER

How do you get a job with one of these great employers? If you've followed the advice so far in the book and are convinced the employer can answer your 'Why should I work for you?' query, then it shouldn't be too difficult. You will already have a good idea of what you can do for this organisation – and that is something the employer will be looking out for. Says Sally Cohen: 'A lot of people are drawn to top employers. And that may be the reason why you *don't* want them. People come to you and say: "I always wanted to work in your organisation." But that's not a reason.

'Top employers don't want someone just looking for a CV builder or someone wanting to join because they admire the brand.'

*Tip: When you're talking to an employer, show how you can add value and make a difference. Indicate that you're not just there to help fill an employment vacancy; you're someone who can grow with the company and be an asset in many ways.*

Kevin Bohan of Diageo concurs: 'We want people who are looking to grow. Who know where they are at and what their aspirations are. We look to recruit people who can potentially move into bigger roles within the organisation and possibly move cross-functionally. We do not want to fill a role just to fill it if it's not the right fit for the

*"We look to recruit people who can potentially move into bigger roles within the organisation and possibly move cross-functionally."*

person and the organisation. We hold the role open until we find the right person.'

That said, if you're the right sort of person then you can find the door to these top employers is wide open. According to Cohen: 'Some top companies even say: "We do not have a job for you but you have the right capabilities and we know we want you in the company. We'll figure out the job later." That's the kind of place I want to work.'

*How to impress a top employer*
- Start with the end in mind. Think about what you want your role to be in five or 10 years' time. How will this job help you get there?

- Think about whether you want to move vertically, through promotion, or horizontally, to get a better breadth of experience. Both might be options.

- Find out why the role hasn't been filled internally. This is a legitimate question if the employer is supposed to have good internal development programmes.

- Ask what your line manager will do to help develop and inspire you and the rest of your team.

- See if you can meet other members of your team to get a sense of their talent levels, backgrounds and education.

*And finally*

You heard the one about Heaven and Hell? A guy dies and is given the choice of which one to go to. So he tries Heaven and has a nice time. Listens to the harp and relaxes. But Hell is fabulous. He has an amazing time playing golf and living the good life. So he tells Saint Peter: 'Hell was pretty damn good, so I'm gonna go there.' And when he goes back down there, it's terrible. All fire and brimstone. He asks the devil: 'What happened?' 'Ah', says the devil. 'When you were down here before you were a recruit; now you're an employee.'

# Bear in mind that if you have talent then an employer will always do its best to impress you. Make sure you get a real sense of its culture before you sign up.

## WHAT NEXT?

If you've stayed with us this far, you should now be on your way to a much happier, more fulfilling job where your skills and abilities will fit in and where you will be recognised and rewarded accordingly. Mission accomplished? Well, almost. But we couldn't bring you this far without making sure you won't stray off the path of a happy work life in one, three or 10 years' time. So before we wave you goodbye, stay with us for one final, and very important, chapter.

*"You should now be on your way to a much happier, more fulfilling job."*

CHAPTER 11:

# Starting well and staying that way

**What you'll get out of this chapter:**
- *Tips on how to get your new career off to the right start.*
- *How to give your new employer a regular appraisal to make sure they're delivering what YOU want.*
- *What to do to keep your work aspirations in line with your changing lifestyle.*

GOT the jitters about starting your new job? Not surprising. Workers in the United Kingdom claim that walking into a new workplace is three times more frightening than getting married. And one in five say it's as scary as a visit to the dentist. No matter how confident you are about having made the right choice, and no matter how much you know about the work from your previous research, the chances are you will be more than a bit nervous about starting your ideal job. And the last thing you want to do is screw up. Here's how to make sure you won't.

> *"Walking into a new workplace is three times more frightening than getting married."*

## FIVE WAYS TO IMPRESS ON YOUR FIRST DAY

- Smile a lot, be sociable and quickly make friends with your new team. In surveys, 48% of people say this is the best way to make a good impression on your first day.

- Show how much you know about your new role and new organisation. If you have done your homework diligently this should not be a problem. Don't overdo it, though. If you go around pretending to know every detail that people are telling you about you will come a cropper sooner or later.

■ Get into the office slightly early or stay until when most other people do, to demonstrate that you're a committed worker rather than a work-shy slacker. Working longer hours when you first start a new job is also a good way of getting to know the people around you, as they're likely to have more time to chat if they're in the office outside of nine to five.

■ Invest in a new wardrobe, if you haven't already done so to attend your interview(s). As we mentioned earlier, you can score a lot of points just on your initial appearance. And if this is a job which you're pretty certain will bring about a positive change in your life, why not reflect that optimism with a great new personal look? It will also make you feel good within yourself and provide you with all-important confidence.

■ Make the tea. Everyone loves a cuppa. And everyone loves someone who makes a cuppa. Plus it's another great opportunity for you to break the ice and get to know your new colleagues better.

*What NOT to do on your first day*
■ Complain about having a hangover.
■ Get drunk in your 'meet the team' lunch do.
■ Fail to recognise your new boss.
■ Insult your new boss.
■ Swear generally.
■ Arrive late for work.
■ Get lost in your new workplace.
■ Spill food or drink down yourself or your colleagues.
■ Call in sick.

## IF THINGS GO WRONG

Once you've got your feet under your new desk (assuming your work involves sitting at one), it should simply be a matter of getting your head down and ploughing ahead with the task at hand. But in some cases, no matter how much painstaking research you carry out beforehand, something goes wrong. This happened to Sally Cohen, the managing director of Elizabeth Arden (UK) whom we met in the last chapter. 'I went to a company years ago and it turned out it was full of bullies,' she says. 'It had never occurred to me to ask about that sort of thing in the interviews.'

If you find yourself facing a similar nightmare, what can you do about it? Consider the following:

1. Stay calm and try to consider the situation dispassionately. Are you blowing things out of proportion? Is this something that can be easily solved with a few minor changes?

2. Find out if your employer has a grievance policy (it should have). Then follow it to try to solve the problem.

3. Make sure you keep all emails, letters and other written documentation relating to the matter. In fact, as a general rule make sure you get in writing anything that relates to your relationship with your employer, including review actions, salary increase notifications and so on.

   *"Get in writing anything that relates to your relationship with your employer."*

4. Try to exhaust every possible internal avenue to resolve a dispute before 'going legal'. Bear in mind that most employers will try as hard as possible to avoid litigation because of the damage it can do to their reputation.

5. In any event, only consider legal action as a last resort. Bear in mind that in most situations the odds will be in your employer's favour.

6. Needless to say, if the relationship with your employer has broken down to the point where you're considering legal action, it's quite unlikely you will continue to work for them. So probably your best strategy is to try to settle things as amicably as possible and then leave.

## IF THINGS GO RIGHT

Hooray! You left your old job, found a much better one, passed the interview, got offered the post … and it's as good as you hoped it would be. How do you make sure things stay that way? Well, here is a simple idea:

celebrate a job birthday. This is basically an annual review of how your employer is performing, and a chance to check that what they're offering is still what you want in terms of your career.

What goes into a job birthday? The simplest way to approach it is to run through a slimmed-down version of the process outlined at the beginning of this book, basically asking 'Why should I work for you?' once more. So:

1. Put yourself through the Happy Days test. How did you score? Are there any areas of concern?
2. Jot down a brief autobiography, incorporating highlights and lowlights of the your new employment. What stands out?

> *"Ask yourself what you have done that you're proud of in your new job in."*

3. Ask yourself what you have done that you're proud of in your new job.
4. Think of your biggest achievement in the job so far.
5. Try to remember when you have felt inspired and/or excited in the role.
6. Cast your mind back to what attracted you to the job in the first place. Do those things still attract you?
7. Remember what was missing from other jobs. Does your current role provide those things?
8. Ask your family and friends whether they feel you have changed since you started the job.
9. Check your original job description. How does it match up to what you're doing now? Did various training, promotion, remuneration promises hold true?
10. Check up on your Jobsite Personal Profile. Remember that these can change over time.

# If you find your new job simply isn't providing a satisfactory answer to the question 'Why should I work for you?', then you know what to do: head back to the beginning of this book!

*When to celebrate your job birthday*
Like your own birthday, try to make your job birthday an annual event. But the timing is up to you. It could be on the anniversary of your joining, or at a time of the year when you're likely to have some time for reflection. Similarly, you could set aside a day, weekend or week to carry out your review, or you could review your situation almost continuously and then decide on what actions you need to take once a year.

One event that it might make sense to try to coincide with is your own employee review, since you will then have the perfect opportunity to discuss any issues with your employer. Whatever you do, though, just make sure you do carry out your review… or in a few years' time you could once again really find yourself asking 'Why should I work for you?'

*Other tips for your job birthday*
Since it's a birthday, why not have a little celebration? Buy yourself a work-related present. Book yourself in for that training session you've been wanting to do for ages. Go out for drinks with your colleagues over lunch or after work. Let your colleagues and your bosses know that you have reviewed your employer. And let them know how the review went. Hopefully it will keep your superiors on their toes. And it might give some of your colleagues some ideas. Hey, here's a thought: why not buy them a copy of this book?

## FROM JOB TO CAREER

If there is one thing you have got out of this book we hope it will be a sense that, as a worker, you no longer need be a passive participant in the job market. The war for talented individuals, the instability of modern organisations and the growing mobility of workers have all conspired to create a situation in which you have a right to seize control of your employment destiny. This book has been about giving you the tools and techniques to do just that. First as a one off, and also, as we have seen with the job birthday, as an ongoing process.

*"You have a right to seize control of your employment destiny."*

Where does this end? Hopefully, the empowerment you've got through this book will ensure that you never again have to suffer at work (or at least not for long). Hopefully, it will also allow you to have a more fulfilling and satisfying career.

## THE REST OF YOUR LIFE

And since your career is a large part of your life, we hope your life, too, will be improved. With your entire career in mind, we leave you with some words of wisdom from Charlie Osmond, a former Unilever staffer who is now the chief executive officer of FreshMinds[42], an executive search business focused on placing high-potential talent in strategy and marketing roles.

'When you look at a job it's always worth thinking about what skills, experiences or contacts you'll have after having been in the role for a few years,' he says. 'Use the interview process to assess what the job, and your line manager, will do for your career. Clearly, a new employer is not looking to recruit someone who is going to walk out the door soon after starting a job, but they'll also recognise that good people can move on. So don't be afraid of asking what external, as well as internal, jobs the role will prepare you for in two or three years' time.

'Also be aware of where certain job decisions may be leading you. If you go into finance, for example, remember that while the rewards may be high, you might not get the same kind of managerial experience that you would in, say, manufacturing.'

A final point, says Osmond, is: 'Be careful of thinking you have to stay on a treadmill too early on in your career. Many people think they have to stay on a particular path once they have started out on it, but you *can* change.'

42. See www.freshminds.co.uk.

Don't do it too often, but by the same token do not be afraid to get out of a rut if you think it's not right for you. Always remember to ask of your employer: why should I work for you?

# References

Stephen J. Dubner and Steven D. Levitt, *Freakonomics: A Rogue Economist Explores the Hidden Side of Everything*, Penguin (2006) ISBN-10 0141019018.

MBTI tests online: see *www.personalitypage.com* or *www.humanmetrics.com*

Marianne Craig, International Coaching Federation master certified coach and director of the Firework Coaching Company, tel: 012 7356 3518, email: *coach@coachlifeandcareer.com*
website: *www.coachlifeandcareer.com*

Michelle Bayley, career coach: tel: 020 8893 9878,
email: *michellebayley@blueyonder.co.uk*
website: *findyourwaycoaching.co.uk*

Marcus Buckingham and Donald O Clifton, *Now, Discover your Strengths*, Pocket Books, (2005) ISBN-10 1416502653; see also *www.strengthsfinder.com*

Dan Ariely, *Predictably Irrational: The Hidden Forces That Shape Our Decisions*, HarperCollins (2008), ISBN-13 9780007256525.

*The Mind Gym: Wake Your Mind Up*, Time Warner Paperbacks, ISBN-10 0316729922.

APPENDIX 1:

# Your happy days scores in detail

This appendix refers to the Happy Days test you took in chapter 1[43]. Make sure you've made a note of the scores you got.

## STRESS

Now, for *stress*, add together all four results from questions 2 and 8. If you get a …

*High score (13–16)*
Your life is not particularly stressful, which is great news. That doesn't necessarily mean that there's no pressure in your life; it could mean that you enjoy it or know how to deal with it.

# Low levels of stress have a positive impact on your health, both directly and indirectly.

Research shows that people with low levels of stress often have strong immune systems, exercise more and drink less alcohol. Try to make sure things stay this way.

*"If you find that things are becoming increasingly stressful at work, don't feel ashamed or embarrassed about speaking to your manager. "*

43. What do you mean, you never took the test? Go back and do it immediately! Or if you're feeling lazy, visit www.jobsite.co.uk/happydays and get the website to do all the calculations for you.

If you find that things are becoming increasingly stressful at work, don't feel ashamed or embarrassed about speaking to your manager. Often problems begin because people around you don't know how you feel. And if you find that you're bringing your workplace stress into your home life, there are also many ways you can deal with your stress. Write down three things you'd like to achieve and allocate at least two hours a week to working on them so that you have a focus outside of work. Or spend at least five hours a week doing your favourite thing – it could be talking to friends and family on the phone, painting, watching films, cooking or whatever.

If possible, budget so you allow yourself a small amount each week or month to treat yourself to something that makes you happy. This could be nothing more than nice chocolates or new make up, or something bigger such as a new sound system or a pair of shoes. Having such treats to look forward to can help with controlling stress. Alternatively, when you get home from work write down in a book all the issues that are bothering you. Don't spend more than half an hour on it. Then close the book and let that be a closure to the issues for the rest of the night.

Finally, consider buying a copy of *The Mind Gym*[44]. It contains advice about dividing your issues into those you can control and those you can't. For those you can't, realise that worrying about them at home is fruitless.

*Medium score (9–12)*
You like to tell yourself that work is not particularly stressful, but inside you know that you're often under pressure. This may mean that you try to hide this from friends and colleagues. Don't. Finding time to talk through issues that are worrying you with people you trust is a proven way to alleviate stress as it can help you gain a broader perspective. Laughter produces endorphins, natural stress-busters, so try to indulge your sense of humour every day. Bottling up stress can have a real impact on your physical and mental health.

Research has shown that people who suffer stress often have weakened immune systems, exercise little and have a poor diet. This can be a vicious cycle. Physical activity is a natural way to relieve stress so leading an

---

44. *The Mind Gym: Wake Your Mind Up*, Time Warner Paperbacks, ISBN-10 0316729922.

unhealthy lifestyle, and turning to alcohol, nicotine or caffeine to cope with stress can all have a negative impact on how the body can cope with pressure.

*Tip: If you find that you're bringing your workplace stress into your home life, there are many ways you can deal with this. Write down three things you'd like to achieve and allocate at least two hours a week to working on them so that you have a focus outside of work. Or spend at least five hours a week doing your favourite thing – it could be talking to friends and family on the phone, painting, watching films, cooking or whatever.*

*If possible, budget so you allow yourself a small amount each week or month to treat yourself to something that makes you happy. This could be nothing more than nice chocolates or new make up, or something bigger such as a new sound system or a pair of shoes. Having such treats to look forward to can help with controlling stress. Alternatively, when you get home from work write down in a book all the issues that are bothering you. Don't spend more than half an hour on it. Then close the book and let that be a closure to the issues for the rest of the night.*

*Finally, consider buying a copy of* The Mind Gym[45]. *It contains advice about dividing your issues into those you can control and those you can't. For those you can't, realise that worrying about them at home is fruitless. If by this stage your stress levels aren't abating and in fact are getting worse then maybe it could be time to start looking for a new job.*

### Low score (4–8)

You're under real pressure in your life. Don't be tempted to bottle things up. Research has shown that people who suffer stress often have weakened immune systems, exercise little and have a poor diet. This can be a vicious cycle. Physical activity is a natural way to relieve stress so leading an unhealthy lifestyle, and turning to alcohol, nicotine or caffeine to cope with stress can all have a negative impact on how the body can cope with pressure.

There are ways to help alleviate stress if you find it's taking over your life. It may sound silly, but make sure you allow for at least one indulgence or pleasure

45. The Mind Gym: Wake Your Mind Up, Time Warner Paperbacks, ISBN-10 0316729922

every day, and actively make time for this. Try to get a burst of fresh air and daylight every day, even if it's only a very short walk. If your levels of work stress aren't improving then it could be time to start looking for a new job.

## BEING IN CONTROL

For *control*, add together all four results from questions 1 and 7. If you get a …

*High score (13–16)*
You're really in control of your life. It could be that you can manage your workload or that you feel that your opinions are valued. As a consequence of this, you may also feel that you have a great balance between your work life and your home life, seldom working late or bringing workplace grievances home with you.

Staying in control depends on how other people view you and how they act towards you. To gain some real insight into this, and to help you stay in control, why not take a look at the Jobsite Personal Profiles in Chapter 3? It will help you to find out a little more about yourself, friends and colleagues, allowing you to manage your relationships with others even more effectively.

*Medium score (9–12)*
You're more or less in control of your life. It could be that you can manage your workload but your working hours mean your home life can be a bit chaotic. Or maybe your home life is under complete control but you sometimes feel that your manager doesn't respect you at work. To help you stay in control at work, it may help to know how other people view you and how they act towards you.

To gain some real insight into this, why not take a look at the Jobsite Personal Profile test in Chapter 3? It will help you to find out a little more about yourself, allowing you to manage your relationships with others even more effectively. Simple steps like sticking to a routine in the

*"Sticking to a routine in the morning or keeping your home neat and tidy will also have a great impact on how in control you feel."*

morning or keeping your home neat and tidy will also have a great impact on how in control you feel.

*Low score (4–8)*
You don't feel at all in control of your life. It could be that you struggle to manage your workload or that you don't feel like your opinions are valued. As a result, you may feel that you can't keep a good balance between your work life and your home life, often having to work late or get in early. To help you stay in control at work, it may help you to know how other people view you and how they act towards you.

To gain some real insight into this, take a look at the Jobsite Personal Profile test in Chapter 3. It will help you to find out a little more about yourself, allowing you to manage your relationships with others even more effectively. Outside of work, you may want to consider ordering your life a little more. Simple steps like sticking to a routine in the morning or keeping your home neat and tidy will also have a great impact on how in control you feel.

## YOUR CREATIVE SIDE

For *creativity*, add together all four results from questions 4 and 9.
If you get a …

*High score (13–16)*
Your life is very creative, with ample opportunities to express yourself. Your job may not be that creative itself, it could just be the way in which you approach tasks. You may also do something very different and imaginative with your leisure time. If your job is not creative itself, why not try to turn your creative pastime into your job? Just be careful that you're not creative to the detriment of other parts of your work. Make sure that you don't spend too much time putting together elaborate presentations, for example, leaving you struggling with your workload.

*Medium score (9–12)*
You think that you have a decent degree of creativity in your life, but do you really? Ask yourself, do your home life and your work life really allow you to

express yourself? If your home life is dull, take the plunge. Think about a hobby or evening class that you've always wanted to do, be it anything from writing a novel to salsa dancing to metal detecting, and do it. And take a good look at your career. Too many people think not only that their work is boring but also that work is supposed to be boring. It doesn't have to be. There could be room within your company for making your job more creative so make sure you ask your manager. You should also ask yourself whether the nature of your work is generally uncreative or if it's how you're approaching it. Consider up-skilling. Often learning new skills can open doors to your imagination.

*Low score (4–8)*
You think that your life is far from creative. Your work life and your home life give you no opportunity to express yourself. If your home life is dull, take the plunge. Think about a hobby or evening class that you've always wanted to do, be it anything from writing a novel to salsa dancing to metal detecting, and do it. Try to spend time in the company of creative people. It frequently rubs off and can lead you into all sorts of creative opportunities you might never have known existed, from writing for a local magazine to stand-up comedy.

> *"Try to spend time in the company of creative people."*

And look for ways that you can stop being a passive consumer of things. Rather than watching TV every night, why not write a blog? It doesn't matter how many people read it. The pleasure of expressing yourself on any subject close to you will give you a real creative buzz, and it may help you take stock of your own life. Finally, take a good look at your career. Too many people think not only that their work is boring but also that work is supposed to be boring. It doesn't have to be.

*Tip: There is probably room within your company for making your job more creative. Ask yourself whether the nature of your work is generally uncreative or if it's how you're approaching it. Try doing the same task in different ways, for instance. Maybe consider up-skilling. Often learning new skills can open doors to your imagination.*

## HOW ARE YOU REWARDED?

For *money*, add together all four results from questions 3 and 6.
If you get a …

*High score (13–16)*
Money is not a problem for you. It may be that you're very well paid, or it may simply be that you earn enough for your needs. Just make sure that the pursuit of money doesn't take over your life. Be sure to read the rest of your feedback and think carefully about whether a position that paid a little less might not greatly improve the overall quality of your life. Earning enough to take extravagant holidays is one thing, but do you have the time to go on them? However much you earn, can you afford to pay the price of added responsibility, stress and unhappiness that may come with it? Perhaps just knowing how much more you earn than other people in your sector will give you a morale boost.

*Medium score (9–12)*
Money is not a great source of concern but it does niggle you. Maybe you feel as though a few hundred pounds a month more would make a massive difference to your self worth or your lifestyle. It can be difficult to talk about money openly, but don't be afraid. Wanting more money is not a sign of greed. It's more a quantifiable indication of how successful you have been and is often a sign of how you want to be respected, how you want to provide for those who are important to you and the type of lifestyle you want. Think about whether money is the real issue.

Is it just improved pay you want, or is it more control over your workload, for your opinion to be heard or greater responsibility? If you cannot earn more in your sector, or with your experience, give serious thought to up-skilling and applying for a better job. If you don't want to leave your current position, consider a hobby or outside activity that could give you a little extra income on the side. In the meantime, take practical steps to make your money go further. Websites such as thisismoney.co.uk and moneysavingexpert.com can help you plan

*"Websites such as thisismoney.co.uk and money-savingexpert.com can help you plan your finances and source great deals and offers."*

your finances and source great deals and offers. Sit down and conduct an audit of your finances. It's a good idea to do this with someone; they can provide a critical eye.

*Low score (4–8)*
Money is a great source of concern for you. It can be difficult to talk about money openly, but don't be afraid. Wanting more money is not a sign of greed. It's often a sign of how you want to be respected, how you want to provide for those who are important to you and the type of lifestyle you want. Think about whether money is the real issue. Is it just improved pay you want, or is it more control over your workload, for your opinion to be heard or greater responsibility?

If you cannot earn more in your sector, or with your experience, give serious thought to up-skilling and applying for a better job. In the meantime, take practical steps to make your money go further. Websites such as moneysavingexpert.com or thisismoney.co.uk can help you plan your finances and source great deals and offers. Sit down and conduct an audit of your finances. It's a good idea to do this with someone as they can provide a critical eye.

## ARE YOU REALLY HAPPY?

Lastly, for *happiness*, add together all four results from questions 5 and 10. If you get a …

*High score (13–16)*
You're really happy in your work, which is great news. You might love what your job entails, approach it with the right mentality, or really get on with your colleagues. Or maybe it's your life outside of work that puts a smile on your face. Whichever, it's likely that one will have a positive impact on the other. Take advantage of your current happiness by thinking about what makes you happy and whether it's permanent or not. Are you working on a specific project that you find satisfying and, if so, how will you feel if that ends? Do certain colleagues make your working day? If so, how would you feel if they left?

Whatever it is, there are some simple steps that can help you ensure that the workplace is enjoyable[46]. If some areas do become less than ideal, don't be afraid to act quickly and head off any negativity. Many people are unhappy at work; make sure you're not one of them.

*Medium score (9–12)*
You're fairly happy with your lot. It could be that you see yourself as content rather than actually happy or unhappy, or maybe your mood changes from day to day. If there is one element of your life that is making you particularly happy, try to embrace it. Likewise, if there is one element of your life that is making you particularly unhappy, try to make a change for the better. If it's work, there are some simple steps that can make the workplace more enjoyable[47]. Also try to establish if it's the nature of your work that makes you unhappy or how you approach it.

Why not try to organise something at least once a week outside work hours that you really enjoy? This will do more than give you a few hours a week in which you're happy. It will provide a focus, as it will be something to look forward to during the rest of the week. And if your home life is making you unhappy, there are many simple ways to pick yourself up. Exercise, making time to meet friends or pursuing a hobby or interest are all proven, natural remedies to make you feel better.

*Low score (4–8)*
You're deeply unhappy. It may be that you're unhappy at work and that is having a knock-on effect in your personal life, or vice versa. Whatever happens, don't fail to address problems like this.

*"You owe it to yourself to be happy."*

You owe it to yourself to be happy. Think about whether it's work or home that is causing you problems. Also try to establish if it's the nature of your work that makes you unhappy or how you approach it. Organise something at least once a week outside work hours that you really enjoy.

This will do more than give you a few hours a week in which you're happy. It will provide focus, as it will be something to look forward to during the rest

---

46. For some examples, see www.jobsite.co.uk/happyatwork.
47. As before, there are some examples at, www.jobsite.co.uk/happyatwork.

of the week. And if your home life is making you unhappy, there are many simple ways to pick yourself up. Exercise, making time to meet friends or pursuing a hobby or interest are all proven, natural remedies to make you feel better.

APPENDIX 2:

# My autobiography

(Two pages for you to jot down your autobiography. Remember to think about the whole of your life, not just what's happened in your career. Think about the experiences you've had that have helped make you who you are. What have been the high points? What about the low points? How did you deal with them? Over to you …)

# Index